D1261051

THE NEW WORLD OF WORK

THE NEW WORLD OF WORK

FROM THE CUBE TO THE CLOUD

TIM HOULNE
AND TERRI MAXWELL

INSPIRE™
ON PURPOSE
Changing Lives With Words

The New World of Work: From the Cube to the Cloud

Book ordering: special discounts are available for quantity sales by corporations, associations and other public entities. Contact the publisher for more details.

Published by Inspire On Purpose™
909 Lake Carolyn Parkway, Suite 300
Irving, Texas 75039
Toll Free Phone 888-403-2727
The Platform Publisher™
www.inspireonpurpose.com

Cover Design by Josh Surgeon
Interior Design by Layla Design
Edited by Sue Mellen

Printed in the United States of America
Library of Congress Control Number: 2012942551

ISBN 10: 0982562276
ISBN 13: 978-0-9825622-7-7

To book Tim or Terri for your next speaking event, or for media inquiries, please contact Promote on Purpose at 800.349.5113 or speaker@promoteonpurpose.com.

An early influence in my first job out of college shaped my career, showed me what it was like to own a business and turned me into the entrepreneur I was destined to become…the Phillips family in Kansas City. Mr. P forever taught me the value of negotiation, and I am grateful for the opportunity to have spent my first few years with one of the original pioneers of the paging and cellular business in a family-owned business. A special thanks to Terri Maxwell, my business confidante and friend who provided the inspiration and motivation to finally put down on paper our ideas on how the world of work was changing. Most importantly, thanks to my wife Kim, who broke new ground when she established a business model leveraging professionals in a virtual environment, and forever changed the way we work. I dedicate this book to all of them.

—Tim Houlne

I'd like to dedicate this book to the early pioneers of the virtual work movement, as well as the thousands of professionals who have made the transition from the cube to the cloud. Your insight, encouragement and passion revived my sense of curiosity about this powerful trend. I'd also like to thank the Inspire on Purpose publishing team for your patience, wisdom and expertise, specifically Michelle Morse, Sue Mellen, Josh Surgeon and Layla Smith. And, thanks to Holly Duffin at Promote on Purpose for the powerful promotional plan. Finally, thanks to Tim Houlne for being a wonderful friend, advisor, writing partner and business pioneer. Here's to the New World of Work!

—Terri Maxwell

CONTENTS

INTRODUCTION

HISTORY IS REPLETE WITH EXAMPLES of economic transformations that, in retrospect, seemed perfectly logical. However, the human beings most directly affected by those changes did not **experience** them rationally. Instead, they experienced those economic course corrections as disconcerting and often terrifying. On the other hand, the people and companies who embraced these transformations often maximized new opportunities, revolutionized industries and created generations of wealth, *all because they could see the benefits of the change, rather than the change itself*.

As the authors of this book, our objective is to help professionals, corporations and business owners negotiate this New World of Work. We are business leaders who have been successful in start-ups, small businesses and large enterprises. Over the last decade we shared a range of market insights with each other about the monumental shift in the way the world works. Although our early grasp of workforce changes were on-target, it was only in the last few years that it became clear we had recognized a revolutionary market-shift—as it was just gathering steam, and before almost anyone understood its impact.

Tim Houlne *has been the CEO of Working Solutions, a premier virtual agent and technology solutions provider, as well as serving on the Board of Directors for Vision Bank of Texas and The Movie Institute.*

Tim has authored multiple articles and white papers covering a wide range of subjects including: Top Traits of High Caliber Agents, Platform as a Service and Contact Center Security—Moving to the Cloud. He is a highly sought-after speaker for industry conferences, business summits and schools. He is committed to helping others embrace new concepts and ideas that improve the lives of working professionals while ensuring excellent bottom-line results. His collaboration on this book is the latest example of that commitment.

Terri Maxwell *provides game-changing insights that transform businesses, people and industries. She is an impactful, passionate leader known for creating successful business models and inspiring the potential of those around her. In a career that spans more than 20 years, Terri has put her talents to work for large and small companies, and is a well-known consultant to small businesses and entrepreneurs seeking to accelerate growth. She has built numerous successful companies, and created an impressive and well-known business incubator, Succeed on Purpose®, Inc. in Irving, Texas.*

She is the author of Succeed on Purpose: Everything Happens for a Reason, *a book teaching how to use life's challenges to uncover purpose. In addition, she has been featured in* The Wall Street Journal, The New York Times, The Dallas Morning News *and* Dallas Business Journal.

Ironically, we both created companies leveraging next-generation work without realizing the magnitude of what was occurring. Once we put our observations together, it became clear that this story had to be told.

We vividly recall the day we knew with certainty that this economic shift would revolutionize everything the world knew about work. The next decision was clear: We had to write a book to educate companies and professionals how to navigate the New World of Work (NWOW).

Ready or not, the future is here, and while it may be scary, this new world is also exhilarating. It offers those who choose to embrace it the opportunity to grow with no boundaries. In creating this map to the new world we have:

- Provided a historical context to this new work perspective
- Clarified, in detail, the trends taking place
- Demonstrated how to take advantage of this new marketplace
- Introduced some early pioneers who have already embraced tenets of the New World of Work

A very well known example of someone with tremendous foresight, who took early action in this new world, was the visionary Pierre Omidyar, founder of eBay.

He was a real pioneer in the NWOW. You can imagine how shocked he must have been when, in 1995, a bidder paid $14.83 for a broken laser pointer on his new online auction site named after his consulting company, Echo Bay Technology Group. When he personally contacted the winning bidder to reiterate that he was, in fact, buying a broken laser pointer, the first customer of eBay told the founder that he collected broken laser pointers and was very happy to have found another for his collection. This was the ultimate, new-world expression of the old saying, "One man's trash is another man's treasure." And Omidyar was smart enough to realize that he could use technology to match people with their treasures—no matter how obscure or far away.

Thus began a revolutionary business that has grown to be an industry unto itself, with a base of fifty-five million buyers in all parts of the world. A more interesting fact, however, from the perspective of the New World of Work, is that eBay has more than 430,000 sellers who now consider eBay their primary source of income. If eBay employed all of these people, it would be the second largest retail employer in the world, right behind the behemoth named Walmart by founder Sam Walton.

How eBay and its incredibly diverse group of entrepreneurs make money from this fascinating virtual marketplace has been covered in detail in any number of other books. However, eBay may be the perfect example of how virtual entrepreneurs and businesses can join forces to generate revenues and livelihoods from the New World of Work.

Buckle your seat belt, and let's explore this new frontier.

010110101001010010101010101010101010101010111010101
01010101001101010101011010110100110101010010101010101
00100110100001010101010101010101000100101010110101100
11011010101010101010101000101010101001010101010
10101010101010101011101010101010101001101010101010110
10111010010101010101010101001001001001010000101010101
01010101000100100100100101010101011010101010101010

SECTION ONE

WHERE DID THE WORK GO?

CHAPTER

1

IT'S IN PLAIN SIGHT AND IT'S UP TO YOU TO FIND IT

THERE'S A POPULAR CHILDREN'S BOOK called *Where's Waldo*, in which the lead character—with his signature red-and-white striped shirt and somewhat goofy expression—is obscured by various collections of people and things. He's hidden, but in plain sight (if you'll excuse the paradox), and it's the young reader's task to locate him in every illustration. By the end of the book, children become adept at locating the enigmatic Waldo in a glance.

We can only hope that this instructional parable reminds us of how the simplest truth can sometimes be obstructed by our need to make things complex. And so it is with the New World of Work. If you want to know where the jobs are, here's a hint: They're in plain sight.

You might call this new, adult game *Where's the Work?* And the stakes couldn't be higher.

The Case of the Disappearing Jobs—Or Not!

In listening to politicians and pundits one might think jobs have disappeared completely. They haven't! They're simply hiding in plain sight where only those who can see the obvious are able to find them.

For example, let's say a big company like IBM sets up operations in a new locale. In the past, the company would have staffed the new facility with a thousand new workers. That meant spending hundreds of thousands (maybe millions) of corporate dollars on office space, equipment and infrastructure, and parking lots. No more! Today the company builds a small facility, staffs it with one hundred or so managers while the remaining positions are sent to the cloud (aka the Internet as a repository of applications and services) to be filled by talent around the globe. Not because the labor is cheaper, but because the labor is more talented, and more eager to compete for this work. That's right; *compete* for the work.

Why would a company such as IBM consider the cloud for its talent needs? Because technology and next-generation work now make it possible for companies to work effectively with skeleton crews onsite and large, competent resources spread across the globe.

And that brings us to an important point. You're right if you think much of the "new" work has gone overseas. Work has spread across the globe because companies can now source talent easily. Meanwhile, talented individuals are able to compete for jobs based on the quality of their work rather than price.

Ironically, this doesn't mean those same jobs aren't also available in the United States, because they are. It's just that most Americans don't realize that this work is available, and many are not prepared to compete for work in this way. Furthermore, most U.S. companies haven't grasped how to capitalize on this new talent war, and only a handful of companies are winning the new talent game. You see, just as prospects are competing for work in the cloud, companies must now compete for the best talent by providing interesting projects at competitive pay.

This is why we wrote this book. *The New World of Work* is both a roadmap for professionals seeking a career in this new world, and a compass for those responsible for developing new talent strategies inside companies around the globe.

The New Revolution

We're in the midst of a new work revolution. Its implications are as far-reaching as those of the Industrial Revolution. Although it lasted from 1750 to 1850, it impacted the way we worked for generations after. The Industrial Revolution—coupled with the impact of the Great Depression—pushed jobs from the farm to the factory. The move from farm to factory, and then to the corporation, resulted in a geographical concentration of workers in cities and suburbs rather than a dispersion of workers on family farms. New industries lived, played and evolved, in part to match the way our society worked. The *way* we worked after the Industrial Revolution ultimately reshaped our entire society.

There have been several mini-revolutions since, but nothing to match the scale of the Industrial Revolution. That is, until now.

No Boundaries: Work Didn't Disappear—It Moved

The ***Information*** Revolution, which has occurred over the last twenty years and has involved an almost unbelievable growth in work-enabling technology, has spawned an entirely new way of ***organizing*** work. This new method is responsible for innovative business models and career opportunities, all with one thing in common: **Today, there are *no boundaries* to work.**

Whether your workforce is on-shore, off-shore, near-shore or virtual, the quality comes from the people, not the location. —*Tim McGrath, Vice President, Customer Service, Office Depot*

Over the last two decades the world has experienced several well-publicized workforce developments. First, it was outsourcing, which led to offshoring. Today there is a ubiquitous transformation of work platforms and talent-sourcing that is revolutionizing not just how and where work is performed, but the *way* business is being done.

This new form of work is leveraging the Information Revolution and, in the process, transforming how and where we work. Today work is certainly moving from the cube to the cloud, but in the process it's creating an entirely new breed of help, and it's transforming work and turning it into a marketplace.

Three New-World Workforce Trends

This transformation, and thus the new work environment, has crystallized three key trends that form the basis of this book. We will fully explore these trends and how you can profit from them later, but briefly want to introduce them here:

Work has been *fractionalized*—Routine work has been broken down into small tasks, and, as a result, most companies will be hiring fewer full-time employees as they outsource those routine tasks as contract projects.

Careers have been *virtualized*—With cloud technology and its capacity to allow companies to leverage intellectual property, work (both contract and role-based) is moving from the cube to the cloud. Professionals can work from anywhere and at any time.

Talent has been *globalized*—As noted earlier, the fractionalization of work and virtualization of careers has made talent truly exportable. Forget offshoring; crowdsourcing means that smart businesses can get talent anywhere, anytime.

Crowdsourcing is fascinating because it combines the natural tendency for humans to collaborate and breaks it into manageable fractionalized work units. This model creates tremendous flexibility for both the worker as well as the employer. —Roger Stiles, Chief Information Officer, Fidelity Personal Investing

---

In this new world there are literally no limits to what, how and where work can be performed. While this is clearly an advantage for those businesses that can adapt, it is an even bigger opportunity for professionals who learn how to compete effectively for this work. And, in a world with no boundaries, learning to compete for this work is paramount.

Throughout the book, we'll show you how to use these trends to position your business or career to compete effectively in a boundary-less world of work. Consider this your playbook for the *game of your life*.

Work, Work Everywhere...

In the *Rime of the Ancient Mariner*, the hero of the poem is dying of thirst while surrounded by an endless ocean of water. The now-famous line, "Water, water everywhere, but nary a drop to drink," is all too appropriate for workers who struggle to take advantage of the new work that surrounds them.

According to the International Labor Organization, as of this printing in early 2013, two hundred million people are out of work globally, with an estimated forty million of those unemployed people residing in advanced societies such as the United States, Japan and Europe. Meanwhile, businesses in those nations lament that they are unable to find qualified workers!

A small percentage of this now-persistent unemployment can be explained by weak demand, but clearly there are bigger problems underpinning the stagnant labor market. Despite elevated unemployment levels, many jobs go unfilled in mature economies because employers can't find the right talent.

In 2011, when U.S. unemployment was at 9%, an MGI (McKinsey Global Institute) survey of two thousand U.S. companies found that 30% of the available positions remained open for six months or more. The reason? Companies couldn't find the required talent. During the same period, 36% of European employers claimed to have difficulty filling roles, and as many as 8% of Japanese companies reported the same challenge.

While technology has enabled a new, virtual universe, the speed of business and technological change has outpaced the ability of many people to adapt, resulting in a **mismatch** between work and the skill required to fulfill demand. So the jobs are there—in fact businesses are crying out to fill them. Prospects for work just need to gain the necessary skills, and attitude, to make those jobs their own.

We'll Be Your Guides

For most, this alternate universe seemed to appear overnight. As two of those who saw it early, at first even *we* didn't grasp the magnitude of the shift or understand the drivers fueling it. On behalf of those ready to embrace this fresh perspective, the new world will usher in opportunities and shifts in the ways we approach business.

We know that such dramatic change can feel disconcerting. Once we realized that next-generation work was bigger than the cloud technology that enabled it, even we were caught off guard. You see, technology certainly has changed work. But it is a new breed of worker that is changing the way business is done. This new breed of worker competes for work anywhere in the world. They are what we call "Virtualpreneurs™"—combining an entrepreneurial spirit with virtual work platforms that match talent to the companies who want to hire them, on a contract basis.

That's why we had to write this book. We felt compelled to explain this new world to the millions of professionals in search of work who are in the midst of many opportunities they do not know exist. We also know that this new talent marketplace is changing the way businesses must compete for help, and in so doing, most companies are left without talent to fill open positions because the majority of qualified folks aren't within a fifty-mile radius of their headquarters.

To grasp next-generation work, it is imperative to understand what—not *who*—moved the cube into the cloud. We'll show you why it's inaccurate (and unproductive) to blame corporations for outsourcing jobs and ripping success from our hands. In the global marketplace, boundaries have vanished and work now moves fluidly around the globe, based on available and passionate talent. This is the effect of a new and ubiquitous trend that has turned work into a marketplace rather than the result of corporations simply trying to increase profits.

In order to truly understand this work ecosystem, we must let go of the need to blame and instead grasp that something much bigger is going on. We can no longer blame corporations or the government for not protecting our jobs. It's time to take advantage of the resources surrounding us, set our fears and angst aside, and prepare for the future.

The fact that you've chosen to read this book is a very good indication that you are ready to get started. Companies who capitalize on these trends will have increased leverage through human capital. And professionals who create new career strategies geared to the new world will find their skills to be in high demand.

In the coming chapters, we will explore new business, career and talent models driven by a cloud-based world and a workforce motivated by its *passion* for the work, rather than the *location* of the job. The real benefit of removing the boundaries to work is that it enables one's passion for work to take precedence. And companies that can capitalize on passion will take a lead role in the coming Talent Revolution created by the NWOW.

If you're ready to exploit next-generation work, and plot a new career strategy for yourself or a talent strategy for your business, then this movement is for you. Welcome to the future.

CHAPTER 2

WHO MOVED MY CUBE?

IT MAY BE TERRIFYING for those caught in the vortex between the old and the new way of work. Most professionals earned the right degrees, responded to the demands of their professions, learned the intricacies of their industries and were rewarded under the old system. It feels like a massive betrayal that this old system is falling away.

The truth is that the cube was moved in part by a new breed of professional. They are skilled and passionate global workers who want the freedom to choose the type of work, rather than choosing a job based on its proximity to their homes. Rather than being hindered by location, they are able to compete based on talent and passion. While most of us were sleeping, they skillfully leveraged cloud and mobile technology and created the New World of Work. And it was their passion for work, rather than some indiscreet evil force, that caused work to seep across boundaries and find its way to this new breed of talent.

Let this chapter be a call to action for those most affected by the new order. Professionals need to reinvent themselves in order to compete in the new, global marketplace. Conversely, companies need to wake up to the reality that competing for the best talent locally will soon be a thing of the past. The best person for a job no longer lives within a fifty-mile radius of your corporation.

Where Have the Good Jobs Gone?

According to Gallup Research, Americans believe that the country's most pressing problem is the lack of good jobs. In an October 2012 Gallup study, more than 60% of Americans surveyed chose either the economy in general or lack of jobs as the country's biggest problem, over healthcare, the environment and even global terrorism. The thirty million Americans who are either out of work or significantly underemployed in the worst recession since the Great Depression are left bewildered, confused and in many cases lost.

But it's not just America reporting these problems. Every industrialized nation in the world is dealing with persistent, systemic unemployment and underemployment. This stagnant job market is chipping away at national resources, citizen satisfaction and pure old-fashioned hope. And, it doesn't appear to be getting better.

The lack of good jobs is truly the most pressing issue in the industrialized world, but this challenge can easily be solved if companies and workers begin to think differently. *The work still exists, but the jobs we once held do not.*

Forget the Cheese. Who Moved My Cube?

After the 2000-2001 dot-com bubble burst, an entertaining book helped displaced employees find their way through the aftermath of the Internet bust, and it became a catchphrase standard in common culture. The book was *Who Moved My Cheese*, by Spencer Johnson.

Unfortunately for those involved, this time it's not just the cheese that moved, but also the restaurant, the farmers' market and the grocery store. Everything is different. For the most part, workers can recognize that something about the job marketplace appears to be different, but most professionals can't put their fingers on what the problem is or where their darned cubes went.

Here's why most workers can't see the opportunities of next generation work: They're looking for the jobs they lost, which in most cases no longer exist.

It's Time to Wake Up!

What the displaced don't realize is this: Not only is that old job not coming back, it has probably been broken into small pieces and sent into the cloud for completion. The truth is that the lost job isn't coming back, at least not in the form it left, because work has been **fractionalized, virtualized and globalized.**

Even traditionally safe careers, such as professional sales positions, have been obliterated in this job recession. According to *US News and World Reports*, 400,000 sales positions have been lost since 2008, but not because the work wasn't available. Many of those sales positions were fractionalized as companies moved sales positions to more efficient channels. These new channels included mobile sales tools and outsourced sales channels where contract labor is abundant.

For professionals looking for work, this notion is hard to accept. Maybe they don't want to admit it, or maybe job-transition groups are simply providing stale advice. Either way, it's just not working.

Global professionals who want to compete in the New World of Work must rethink their careers and begin the long road of rebranding and reinventing themselves. Like it or not, everything has changed.

The truth is, in the social/digital decade ahead of us (you know the one, where technology changes in an instant), jobs will change just as quickly. Professionals who want to thrive in this new environment have to think differently. The online virtual-work market reached more than $1 billion in 2012 alone, and it's predicted that a massive one-third of the global workforce could be hired online by 2020. Some reports argue that it could be as high as 50% of the global workforce.

Take This Job and Move It

Let's explore a few roles that have changed in the last four years, to help you better understand the cloud-based world around us:

Administrative Assistants: Once a staple of corporate luxury, administrative assistant jobs have been declining for a decade. Today, those jobs are easily crowdsourced to the tens of thousands of virtual assistants who now work from home. For those not as familiar with this term, crowdsourcing is defined as the practice of obtaining needed services, ideas or content by soliciting contributions from a large group of people and especially from the online community rather than from traditional employees or suppliers. As *Time* noted in an article about the crowdsourcing phenomenon, "We're looking at an explosion of productivity and innovation, and it's just getting started, as millions of minds that would otherwise have drowned in obscurity get backhauled into the global intellectual economy."

According to Marketwatch.com, businesses trying to weather the economic downturn are turning in huge numbers to virtual Business Process Outsourcing (vBPO), outsourcing that involves contracting specific business functions or processes to third-party companies or individuals. That means that they're looking online to hire thousands of people for support positions in their organizations. According to the Q2 2012 survey by Freelancer.com, hiring of virtual assistants increased by 18% to 3,770 jobs during the quarter, demand for MS Word processing skyrocketed 119% to 1,594 jobs, and data processing hiring was up 16% to 21,274 jobs. Hiring of people with skills in Excel was up 13% to 22,947 jobs.

Professionals: Professionals' jobs didn't go overseas this time. Instead, they went into the cloud and to other professionals working from home. According to IBIS World, the number of temporary workers in the U.S. is on the upswing, and will continue to increase at least through 2017, reaching 3.5 million.

Engineers and Programmers: As technology has become more streamlined, so have the ways in which it's programmed, designed and engineered. Companies have moved this work into the cloud through such brands as Amazon, Google, Genesys, Oracle, Hewlett-Packard, Microsoft and a host of others, including EMC, Cisco and Red Hat. That translates to a range of cloud-related development jobs—often from remote locations—for engineers and programmers.

Project Managers: Do you know that there are more contract jobs available to you on Elance.com and oDesk.com than there are physical project management jobs available on recruiting job boards across the U.S.?

According to an online employment report on Elance.com, the company posted 197,000 jobs in the second quarter of 2012. Online employment is a one billion dollar industry comprised of companies with online platforms for hiring contractors. It's in double-digit growth mode driven by global expansion and favorable workforce trends.

Marketers: Your industry has been obliterated because of the double whammy of the job recession coupled with new social and digital-marketing strategies unfolding each and every day. Your profession was listed as Number Two in the list of Top 10 Dying Careers in the June 2011 *Forbes* article "The Disappearing Middle Class." But don't despair! You can take your skills to the cloud and find a global network of companies who want to hire American marketers trained in famously effective American marketing strategies.

Let us be clear: This isn't an attempt to scare you and cause panic. Instead, it is meant to inform professionals so they will understand that the work still exists, just in a different form.

And it means that it's time to think differently. The old job system is disintegrating before our eyes, and it's being replaced by platforms that give professionals powerful new options for taking their passions and skills to market. Gone are the days where we have to accept management styles like those mocked on *The Office*, and long commutes followed by even longer work hours. Today, we can create our own jobs. We can put together work streams of projects that we enjoy, rather than being forced to do tasks simply because they are considered part of the "other-duties-as-assigned" aspect of our job description.

Presently, professionals can freelance skills through Elance, Freelancer, Working Solutions or oDesk. For passionate graphic designers, there's LogoTournament.com and 99Designs.com, both of whom are actively seeking designers, copywriters and marketing professionals to compete openly for projects and be paid based on the quality of work rather than the time spent doing it.

In this new world, the worker is in control of the work they select, the hours they work and work choices that are built around their lifestyle.
—*Rich Peterson, Chief Marketing Officer of Elance*

Even the HR Department Can't Find the Cube

Just look at any job-posting board and observe the manic trend played out. One week a company advertises for a marketing communications specialist. A week later that job is pulled down, and now the company wants a PR manager. Then, a few weeks later, that job disappears and the same job is titled social media specialist.

What's the deal? Why does the same job have three different titles? And it's not just occurring in marketing; the phenomenon is occurring in IT, sales, finance and operations. So what is going on?

Yesterday's jobs don't exist, and tomorrow's career options are changing quickly. As a result, most companies are caught between their old way of sourcing talent and these next-generation work models.

So both business leaders and working professionals are frantically looking for once-earthbound jobs. The fact that they can't see them doesn't mean they no longer exist; they have simply moved.

Work Has Moved into the Cloud

Here's how dramatically the job marketplace has changed: Currently, work opportunities are more readily available virtually than locally. And most of the new virtual work options are contract jobs with performance pay, rather than the archaic and bureaucratic work system that compensated employees with wages and benefits for time well spent, rather than work well done.

Since a large portion of the work is being redistributed through contracts on virtual work platforms, those countries whose citizens access these platforms will win the jobs war, because that's where the work can be found. According to *Financial Times*, as it turns out, prospects from developing markets are capitalizing on virtual workforce trends. India, Pakistan, Bangladesh, Ukraine and the Philippines are among the top providers of virtual workers, with millions of hours of brainpower exchanged every day on the Web. The result is what the publication refers to as "impact sourcing," which is increasingly becoming an important source of income in these countries.

CONTRACTORS BY COUNTRY

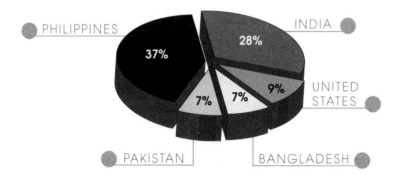

Source: *Financial Times,* Elance and oDesk

And, as virtual collaboration tools and mobile technology improve, virtual work will become easier for a hyper-available workforce digitally connected.

So, if the United States—AND ITS WORKERS—want to win the job war, we must rethink the concept of work. Jobs have moved from the cube to the cloud, and the countries whose professionals capitalize on this trend will win the talent war.

You Can Win This War

For professionals who are left confused by the new talent market, the critical shift that must be made is to stop looking for jobs, and to think more about work. You should be asking yourself:

- What type of work am I most passionate about?
- How do I prefer to work?
- What type of company and culture appeals to me?
- In what roles can I be effective?

Professionals who want to compete in this constantly changing environment have a huge advantage if they can stop worrying about their job and build a new career strategy. *This book is designed to give professionals a map to this new world, whether that professional is a hiring manager, a corporate executive trying to develop a competitive talent strategy or a job seeker stuck between worlds.* Without boundaries, skilled help is free to compete in new ways, and companies will compete for talent and maximize their future (and profits) one worker at a time.

So, what does tomorrow's workforce look like? What will be changed? What will remain the same? What are the trends and how can we capitalize on them? We briefly introduced the three key trends in Chapter One, but let's take a closer look at them individually, learn what they mean for our economy and find out why we should care. Understanding how these new trends have removed work boundaries is critical to maximizing the New World of Work.

Let's explore these trends and begin to understand the roadmap to the New World of Work.

THREE WORKFORCE TRENDS

THE TRANSFORMATION that created the New World of Work is being driven by three key trends:

WORK HAS BEEN FRACTIONALIZED...

CAREERS HAVE BEEN VIRTUALIZED...

TALENT HAS BEEN GLOBALIZED...

Most professionals have suspected that something has changed about the world of work. As we faced the current job recession and economic downturn, many sensed something bigger at play. However, until now, it wasn't clear what the transformation was. The future is here, whether we are ready or not.

Where Did the Work Go?

In 2009, a single question prompted us to research the talent marketplace, which ultimately led to the formation of this book: When the U.S. economy lost eight million jobs, and the global economy lost millions more, we asked ourselves, "Where did the work go?"

Not where did the people go, which is what the media and the government focus on, but where did the actual *work* go?

Even more curious, the majority of those "jobs" still have not been replaced five years later, yet business profitability has recovered in all but a few countries. So where did the actual work go?

Believe it or not, the work wasn't outsourced. Every industrialized country seems to have a similar labor situation: higher than usual unemployment, profitable businesses and a high, yet unfulfilled demand for talent.

So, where is the actual work located?

In order to answer the question of where the work went, we must first understand what happened to the *way* we worked.

Trend 1: Work Has Been Fractionalized

Fractionalized work means that routine tasks (administration, project management, medical transcriptions, basic programming, and so on) have been broken down into small pieces and bundled together. That makes sense, but why haven't we added some of these jobs back? Why are there still high rates of unemployment in administrative and project management professions?

The fundamentals of economic flow suggest that all markets will eventually find the most efficient path toward maximum utilization. For professionals, that means there is a new talent *marketplace*, and a more efficient way to perform work than in the traditional job models of the past. This fact, coupled with the fractionalization of work, has enabled the next two trends to be realized.

Trend 2: Careers Have Been Virtualized

What does it mean to virtualize work? Quite simply, it involves using new virtual technology to support a contingent, remote workforce. Many of the routine tasks that were performed in corporate cubes can now be performed virtually, from anyone's computer, and predominantly in home offices around the globe.

Quick, name one of the fastest growing companies in the world? Google? Sure. Apple? Yes. What about oDesk?

Most professionals and business leaders haven't even heard of oDesk. That's unfortunate, because oDesk built one of the fastest growing talent marketplaces by linking corporations with *virtual* talent to fill work gaps on a contract basis. oDesk, which is a shortened version of the words "online desk," allows companies to post freelance projects on its platform at no cost. Freelance contactors are allowed to post profiles and bid on projects also for no charge. And, oDesk isn't the only virtual work platform experiencing record growth. There are many more, including Elance.com and Freelancer.com.

Most of these Virtual Work Platforms retain 10% of the fees generated by matchmaking "projects" to "talent," and also supply both the bookkeeping and collaborative software, which both parties need to effectively communicate during the process. As of 2012, oDesk reported that it had about 350,000 hiring firms worldwide, and 2.3 million contract workers on its platform. By New-World-of-Work standards, oDesk could easily be considered one of the largest employers in the world.

Its largest competitor, Elance, operates in a similar fashion, with a few competitive advantages. Elance made a strategic decision to guarantee workers payment by using an innovative escrow system. It collects payment in advance and holds it in escrow until the work is completed. This unique model basically guarantees the virtual worker that he/she will receive payment, but it also ensures the hiring company only pays for completed work. As a result, it claims to get better jobs, and better talent. Elance is growing 40% per year and prides itself on turning the workplace into a marketplace.

The virtualization of careers is good news for the economy for a number of reasons:

- Professionals who choose to embrace this new virtual career model will find plenty of work.

- According to Telework Research Networks, businesses that let one hundred employees work half of their time from home can save more than $1 million a year, freeing up more money for capital investment and expansion. Clearly, companies can save even more when a major part of the workforce is completely virtual.

The trend toward the virtual workplace has changed everything—for businesses, workers, and landlords, who are renting much less space. Now businesses can save on things like brick-and-mortar costs and employee commutes. When you eliminate a commute you save twenty to thirty minutes on each end of an employee's day plus their transportation costs. It's like you gave them a raise and more free time. —David Litman, CEO, Getaroom.com

---

Companies can find better talent virtually, without borders, simultaneously increasing profitability, productivity and worker satisfaction. *What business wouldn't sign up for that?*

However, for those professionals and workers who fail to recognize the opportunities of virtualization, this is not good news. This leads us to the third trend.

Trend 3: Talent Must Be Globalized

If work has been fractionalized, and careers have been virtualized, talent is now globalized, whether we like it or not. It is now more efficient to find talent globally than it is to search in the confines of a fifty-mile radius of the corporate headquarters.

Just look at any number of corporate headquarters of international companies. What was once a beehive of activities—floor after floor of project management teams, financial analysts, marketing teams, accounting teams and all of the other professionals who are critical in getting the work completed—now sit empty.

How did this happen?

Quite simply, the work **moved.**

When work moved from the farm to the factory in the early 1900s, it required centralized workforce models. Those companies that adopted new models gained a strategic advantage by leveraging the centralized workforce.

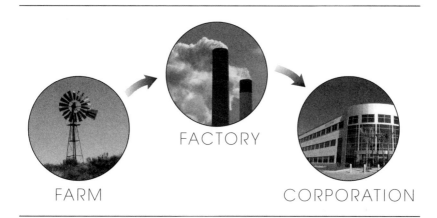

FACTORY

FARM   CORPORATION

The reverse is true today: Routine work is more effectively performed in a virtual decentralized model. Because human capital has moved from the cube to the cloud, talent can be found virtually, regardless of country of origin. This isn't about "jobs going overseas," it is about a new way of working that strikes at the heart of everything we once knew about work.

Smart companies can leverage the talent marketplace with literally no boundaries, and clever professionals can use the cloud to effortlessly take high-demand skills to this new market.

Virtualization, like a wave crashing on the shore, picked up the work in its wake, and dispersed it across the globe. Virtualization isn't just about the Internet; it's really the intersection of a range of enabling technologies and trends, and furthermore, it's a convergence of technology.

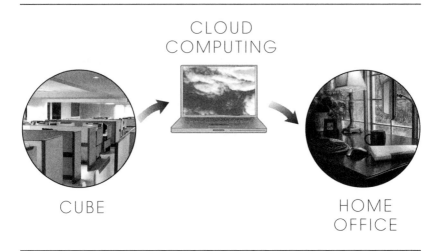

CLOUD
COMPUTING

CUBE

HOME
OFFICE

Convergence: A Technological Shift

To better grasp how the three trends affect our interaction in the workplace, let's look at some of the factors that drove change. The Information Revolution driven by technology was like an earthquake that began the shift to the New World of Work. But the seismic shift that followed, and what is really powering this workforce transformation, is a technological shift known as Convergence.

Convergence isn't about the Internet; the Internet boom in the late nineties wasn't the real innovation. It was the *access to information* the Internet enabled that spawned a new revolution and created the **no-boundaries** environment of the New World of Work.

Rather than the Internet alone, it is the convergence of *more than one technology* that is enabling this new way of work. On many levels, it's historically similar to the convergence of steam technology and steel manufacturing, which propelled the Industrial Revolution and created the factory-centric model of work. Without the simultaneous development in the iron and steel industries, advances in the early steam engines would not have been possible. As steam-powered rail transportation flourished, the transport of finished goods was more affordable.

The cheaper transportation resulted in more demand, thereby stimulating more expansion in factories and more use of iron and steel in the manufacturing of goods. That's how the convergence of the steel and steam industries became the linchpin for the Industrial Revolution, which powered the last radical work force makeover, when work moved from the farm to the factory.

Today's technological convergence is more than transportation enablement: Convergence is based on transformational technologies *simultaneously* converging in the inflexible corporate structure. Each advance in technology enables faster and faster knowledge processing, creating global access to information at our fingertips. More importantly, every day these technologies simultaneously converge atop one another, exponentially multiplying to transform everything we do.

THE CONVERGENCE OF CLOUD COMPUTING, MOBILE, AND SOCIAL

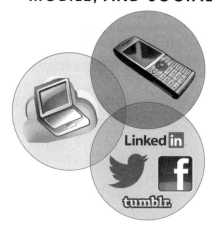

The core technologies that are converging in corporate infrastructure are:

- Cloud Computing (Software as a Service and Platform as a Service)
- Social Media
- Mobile Technology

Social and Mobile Technologies Breed Exponential Power

The power of convergence isn't just these technologies operating independently; it's the simultaneous impact they are creating on the corporate and community structures. Let's look briefly at each, and then combine their effects.

Cloud computing is hot, but what's really heating up is the empowerment of small businesses and global *solopreneurs* who no longer need expensive infrastructure to compete. Businesses can have world-class interaction and transaction infrastructure for a small fee per month, per license. A start-up can have a sales force automation system, a project management system, an accounting/finance suite and a world-class customer relationship management system *combined* for less than $100 per month.

I also see the growing use of avatars to initiate collaborative problem solving, with live experts brought in as needed, to help clients deal with support issues. Leveraging search technology and artificial intelligence, avatars can assist clients in finding known solutions to problems. My support vision is to have humans work on only new problems; let automation and advanced systems resolve existing problems when they occur.
—Mike Runda, Senior VP and President, Avaya Client Services

Why would any company not use the power of the cloud?

As cloud computing is making its way into our business toolkit, social media is changing the relationship between companies and their customers. Gone are the days when advertisements told us what to buy. Now our *friends* tell us what's in, and what products and companies to avoid.

More news is delivered through social media than on TV and radio combined. Virtual bloggers are replacing broadcast news analysts, which is why that profession was also listed as one of the Top 10 Dying Professions according to the 2011 article "Disappearing Middle Class Jobs" in *Forbes* magazine.

Then, there's mobile. The power of this tool is not just the ability to talk on the phone, but also the ability to **transact** on the phone. More transactions, from purchases on Amazon.com to orders for Domino's Pizza, are moving to mobile phones, without any human interaction to up-sell or cross-sell. It's all done electronically. In 2010, it was rare to see someone authorize your credit card on a smart phone. Today it is an everyday occurrence.

A good example of convergence is as close as your smart phone. Each day, millions of people around the globe—in highly industrialized areas and even third-world villages—use their mobile phones to **transact** business. This has created incredible opportunities for companies that have developed the infrastructure to capitalize on mobile transactions. To put the new world in context, the mobile payments industry did not exist a few years ago. Yet today, the growing accessibility of mobile commerce is wreaking havoc for governments accustomed to clear borders for e-commerce taxation, and is quickly becoming the source of government scrutiny around the globe.

Mobile transactions are the epitome of the power of a convergence-driven marketplace that rips down borders and removes boundaries, irrespective of legislation or regulation. And, in this new world, finding talented people who can develop mobile commerce strategies is as easy as www.elance.com. Go to the site and up pops a list of virtual professional profiles with skills in the development of mobile commerce. It's that easy.

Furthermore, the real power of convergence is the *simultaneous* impact of these technologies, which is reshaping the way we do business.

Here is a hypothetical situation sequence of events that could impact even the corporate monolith Microsoft. Imagine that Google launches a new word-processing tool on Monday. By Friday, a solopreneur in Bangladesh releases a mobile application of that same tool. Two weeks later, another start-up develops a cloud-based platform to replace the need for Microsoft Word completely. Say good-bye to the venerable Microsoft Word.

Convergence is like one of those airborne viruses that science fiction stories favor. It literally comes blowing in before we actually see it, wiping out everything in sight.

Why You Should Care

Yes, the NWOW is here, and the boundaries have been ripped apart by a tidal wave known as convergence.

So, why should we care? Why should we pay attention?

The companies that capitalize on these new trends will gain huge strategic talent advantages, lower costs and improve expertise. And the professionals and employees of these companies will make themselves even more valuable and create totally new career models that we haven't even thought of yet.

For the corporation, the entrepreneur, the solopreneur and the professional, there is one fundamental truth: Today's job will not exist in five years, and tomorrow's job hasn't been created yet. The only thing we have is the opportunity to capitalize on this dynamic, and take no boundaries to the next level.

Randy Rubingh, Customer Service Director at StubHub, Inc., is interested in only empowered workers to staff his company's call centers.

*"These days we need more educated, skilled people to handle the level of difficulty in transactions," he says. In StubHub's case, customers purchase their tickets online. So the interaction when a customer **actually calls** is more detailed and requires service, communication and problem-solving skills. Hence the need for more educated, articulate customer service agents. For example, customers now want to know 'Where's the parking? Where exactly are these seats? Can I upgrade my tickets?' A knowledgeable person has to be available to answer these type questions."*

Randy notes that in just a few years StubHub has gone from 0% virtual workers to about 20% virtual, and he expects that percentage to double in the next few years.

"The distributed/virtual workforce is becoming much more the norm. Companies have to do it to remain competitive. This is the shape of the workplace of the future," he says. Rubingh believes that the New World of Work is characterized by a number of traits, including:

- *The ability to capitalize on talent in a national work pool instead of a region enhances your competitive advantage.*

- *To get the bright, articulate people, the key is expanding the geography to access the best labor pool.*

- *Lower attrition means providing flexible work schedules and an environment that attracts smarter people.*

"The advances in technology, the flexibility and the growing acceptance of the virtual agent has attracted a much more capable, mature and qualified candidate. SERVICE truly comes down to PEOPLE and it's crucial to have the right people available to keep customers satisfied," he concludes.

It is important to understand that the power of convergence isn't about big business, big government or even the global talent marketplace. What is powering these workforce trends is the simultaneous ALIGNMENT between the empowered workforce and the empowered customer. Both have whole new sets of tools and are ready to take control.

Tomorrow's workforce has indirectly partnered with today's customers and demands one thing: to be empowered.

CHAPTER

4

THE EMPOWERED CUSTOMER

IN ADDITION TO EMPOWERED WORKERS, there is another force fueling the New World of Work: Convergence has also empowered the customer. Every business model since the birth of free enterprise has been centered on customers. If a new model were created to transform business, it would only work if customers also benefited. Truly disruptive business models are created when the customer becomes the catalyst for change. Just look at the recent advent of digital music or smart-phone technology. Not only was the customer considered in R&D analyses, but in many cases customers actually drove product innovation.

A perfect free-market economy organizes what is produced or designed according to customer demand. The customer has and always will dictate what she wants and on what terms, and a business that understands what customers want will win the battle for their discretionary spending. Today's consumers are becoming more demanding and less loyal to traditional brands because they are empowered. In its 2011 Global Consumer Research Study, research consultancy Accenture found that "only one in four consumers feels 'very loyal' to his or her providers across industries, and just as many profess no loyalty at all. Furthermore, two-thirds of consumers switched providers in at least one industry in the past year due to poor customer service. Forty-four percent of consumers said their expectations today are higher than they were just a year ago."

Today, *as never before*, the customer has a new set of tools to communicate. With social media, customers can provide instant feedback on likes and dislikes, and do it in full, open view of the entire marketplace, rather than behind a smoked glass window with researchers analyzing feedback. Customer research is now as simple as reading the Facebook, Twitter, Yelp or Pinterest post of any company brave enough to put a page into cyberspace. Whether making a Facebook post or setting up a boycott of a specific company's website, customers know they have the power to force companies to respond. The tables have turned in this new world, and the customer clearly has control.

Perfecting Customer Service

As one of the best-known and successful online retailers, Amazon deals with literally thousands of customer service challenges every hour. While the volume of customer service queries is not that unusual for a company of this size, it is the way that Amazon deals with these queries that makes it stand out. The company states its philosophy simply: "Customer experience is more than customer service."

In a *Bloomberg Business Week* article that dealt with Amazon's approach to customer service, it was noted that a customer had been "ripped off" on a purchase by someone selling his own goods through Amazon. Rather than arguing about who was right and who was wrong, Amazon refunded all of the money to the offended customer, even though she was not paying Amazon directly for purchased goods. The customer was quoted in the article as saying that she felt that Amazon was "standing up for her."

This story and others about Amazon's superior customer service have been spread rapidly through blogs, consumer websites and traditional media such as *Business Week*. As a result, positive digital "word-of-mouth" feedback has rewarded Amazon with record-setting growth, while equally punishing other firms who were not customer-centric.

Beyond Customer Service

With an empowered customer in a position of strength, companies are now viewing customer service as a primary differentiator. Labeled as "delivering a branded experience," businesses in every industry are stepping up efforts to provide superior customer service. And right on cue, the customer has become more demanding.

And, the demands are quite intriguing. These empowered customers don't just want great service; they want an integrated customer service *experience*, whether they call into a customer service center, send an email, make a Facebook post or tweet or conduct an online chat session. Multi-channel communication is now part of our daily lives, so the company that makes the customer's life easier, more convenient and more organized through fully connected access to the company, will win the hearts of the empowered customer.

Probably the best example of avant-garde customer experience is online shoe retailer, Zappos. Asked frequently how they've grown so quickly, they note that the secret to their success is quite simple:"Customer service isn't a department, it's a way of doing business." The entire company is built *around* the customer.

Zappos offers free returns with a "no questions asked" policy. Okay, easy enough.Where's the revolution?Well, it's the little examples of extraordinarily great customer service that have become Zappos folklore.

- In 2011, a Zappos employee sent flowers to a customer who ordered six different pairs of shoes because her feet were damaged by harsh medical treatments.The employee who sent the flowers felt like the customer needed something to lift her spirits.

- In 2012, a customer service team member physically went to a rival shoe company to get a specific pair of shoes for a woman staying at the Mandalay Bay hotel inVegas because Zappos ran out of stock.

- Also in 2012, Zappos overnighted a FREE pair of shoes to the best man of a wedding party because he had forgotten to pack his shoes.

However, Zappos' website isn't drenched in self-praise. Instead, customer comments are clearly posted for the world to see. And the company posts all comments, not just the positive ones. Furthermore, good luck trying to find executive bios. The company Family page is focused on department teams and how they serve, rather than cold headshots of corporate executives who sit in an ivory tower and dictate the company's growth strategy.

Tony Hsieh, the visionary CEO of Zappos, explains how an emphasis on corporate culture can lead to unprecedented success. Some of the suggestions he offers in his best-selling book, *Delivering Happiness*, include:

- Paying new hires $2,000 to quit if they're not happy at Zappos, figuring it costs more to employ unhappy employees (called "The Offer")

- Building customer service into the entire company (rather than a separate department)

- Focusing on company culture as the Number One priority

- Applying research from the science of happiness to running a business

- Helping employees grow both personally and professionally

- Seeking to change the world and making money at the same time

The company is consistently ranked among the top companies to work for in the world by *Fortune* magazine, and was acquired by Amazon in 2009. Currently, Zappos.com is closing more than $1 billion in gross merchandise sales every year, all because they built their entire business model around the customer.

Technology Enabled the Customer

The coolest part of Zappos customer-centric culture is the access it provides to any team member at any time, through any channel. You can literally reach any department through a tweet, a Facebook comment or the company's website, in addition to its call center.

Zappos *understands* these empowered new customers who demand 100% wired access, 100% of the time, meaning they want access by every means possible at any time. This is the new requirement for their discretionary spending. No longer is this a nice-to-have differentiator. Total access has become what we like to call table stakes to the empowered customer.

Unlike many technology innovations of the past, the digital age has empowered the customer as fast as it has corporations and leagues of personnel. At home, consumers and businesses have access to social, mobile, video and cloud services including Facebook, Android, iPad, Foursquare, Google, YouTube, Office web Apps and Twitter; the list is endless and growing every day. Empowering technologies like these have never been made so readily available to users. This technology puts tremendous power directly into the hands of customers, who are happy to use it.

There is one constant of technology: it changes all the time. With this change, so goes customer demand. Customers have rapidly become accustomed to instant telephone and electronic communication, and the ability to watch television programs on-demand.

Customers often have more information than a company's sales team or support staff. They can also wallop brands from their smart phone, with video even, while waiting impatiently in line for the company's employees to answer their questions. They can get recommendations from people in their business networks while listening to advertising or sales pitches. Businesses must face the facts—the customer has control.

SoundBite believes the customer has to be in charge, because they will pick the channel they want to buy from as easily as they select the product. With the commoditization of many products, the only way most brands can differentiate is by providing a better customer experience. That means that providing a great experience, regardless of what medium a customer uses to communicate with your brand is essential. —Jim Milton, CEO of SoundBite Communications (SoundBite Communications (SBDT), a leading provider of multi-channel customer experience management software, innovating new ways for customers to put the customer in charge)

Successful Employees Will Have Customer-Centric Tools

Over the past ten years, customers have obtained the means to find products through search tools such as Google, Bing and a large variety of others before the brands advertise them. These new tools make it easier for customers to reach out to their peers for feedback via social networks and word-of-mouth prior to spending one dime, regardless of any company-sponsored advertising.

Customers are empowered by information and connections, and they are ready and willing to use it. So, what does this have to do with the changes in the workplace? At the heart of the talent marketplace rests the empowered customer.

Future job creation will differ dramatically from those in the past. Prospects with strong communication, analytical and problem-solving skills are in hot demand for one very important reason: For businesses to serve an empowered customer, they must have capable employees who can directly engage the needs and expectations of the empowered customers.

And only empowered employees can solve the problems of empowered customers. Employees who think critically and communicate effectively will be in demand for tomorrow's jobs.

The empowered customer has been gaining momentum over the last decade, and now social media has launched them to even greater heights. Instantaneous, real-time feedback is available anywhere, anytime on any product or service. Do you see the correlation to how people work anywhere, and at anytime, on anything they desire? This similar, complementary overlay between the customer and the service provider will create powerful opportunities for both segments, while changing the way each interacts.

It is easier now than ever before in the history of free enterprise or consumerism to express frustration or disappointment with a product or service. More importantly, it is easier than ever before to tell other consumers about your experience.

The same holds true for products or services that exceed one's expectations. Customer feedback has become the most trusted form of consumer-behavior influence. By tapping into this jet stream of positive exposure, a brand can reap the benefits of the empowered customer.

If empowered customers are driving the push toward the New World of Work, the professionals who serve them are providing the fuel. Good jobs that are both personally fulfilling and critical to business success are waiting for those who understand the new dynamics of this environment.

In order to understand the new cloud-based work model, we must first dissect the fractionalization of work, understand the needs of the future workforce and focus on the types of jobs best suited for virtualization and globalization.

Zappos is just one example of a business that is helping to transform the business landscape, and is thus transforming the way people work. In the next chapter, we'll look at how workers have changed and what really motivates the new, virtual workforce. (Here's a hint: It's not about money anymore!)

010110101001010010101010101010101010101010111010101
010101010011010101010110101101001101010010101010101
001001101000010101010101010101010001001010110101100
110110101010101010101010100010110101001010010101010
101101010101010101110101010101010100110101010110
1011010011010101010101010101001011010000101010110101
010010100101010101010101101010101010101010101010

SECTION 2

WORK: FRACTIONALIZED

CHAPTER

5

MOTIVATING TOMORROW'S WORKFORCE

THE NEW WORLD OF WORK is a fundamental shift in the way people work, changing organizations and disrupting the manner in which businesses operate. It will be a driving force in the new global economy of the future, enabling a new form of competition like never before. Those who embrace it will thrive, while those who don't will become extinct.

To explore each of these new work trends—the fractionalization of work, the virtualization of careers and the globalization of talent—it is important to understand that they work together, like parts of a well-oiled machine.

Fractionalization is now possible because we have the virtualization of careers and the globalization of talent. It is the trifecta combination of business demands creating the need for fractionalized work, as well as workers making a purposeful shift towards the benefits of a virtual career. This, of course, is then followed by technology simultaneously enabling both the virtualization of work and the globalization of talent.

Technology blew down the barriers, but in many cases it is the professionals who created their own careers that ultimately moved work from the cube to the cloud.

Said another way, technology equipped the customer to be more demanding and enabled work to be performed anywhere. But this new freelance, virtual worker, who demands to work on his own terms, is truly powering the new machine of work. The combination of these factors—technology, the empowered customer and the freelance virtual worker—is truly changing the way business is done.

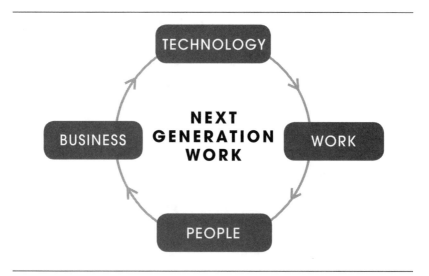

To comprehend the fractionalization of work, we must understand the willingness of the workforce to adopt this new model, as well as the marketplace that enabled it to occur. There are three societal drivers that create a three-hundred-sixty-degree connection between the fractionalization of work and virtualization of careers:

    1) Motivation: There is a global talent pool driven more by quality-of-life than traditional compensation structures.

2) Productivity: This same global talent pool that demands high-quality work at decent wages has been equipped to work from home, regardless of the origin of work. Not only are these prospects more capable, but in many cases they are more productive. A recent, randomized study by researchers at Stanford University compared productivity rates of a company's onsite workers with remote workers. During the nine-month study, the researchers found a 12% increase in productivity for the at-home workers. Of that increase, 8.5% came from working more hours (due to shorter breaks and fewer sick days) and 3.5% came from more performance per minute. The researchers speculate this was due to quieter working conditions.

3) Market Demand: All markets move towards optimum efficiency. In the case of work, the new talent marketplace can enable companies to more efficiently compete. As a result, there is growing market demand for higher quality and specialized skill sets found in the virtual talent marketplace.

It's clear that—given the right qualifications and support—workers are more productive in home offices, often by several percentage points. Dan Bell, President and CEO, Mobile America.

The combination of these three drivers is fueling the demand for fractionalized work.

To comprehend the nature of fractionalized work, let's explore the origins of productive work: the process of creating or producing value, also known as a *job*. Just as the work performed satisfies a need for a business, the activity of *creating value* satisfies a need for the individual who performs the work. Work production also creates value for the individual completing the work: a *reward*. In the study of sociology, rewards are considered economic preference functions, because the preference for rewards is different for various population segments and these preferences change over time. For virtual workers, the new contingent workforce, there is a different set of economic preferences than their predecessors who moved from the factory to the corporation and ultimately into the cube.

So What Does All That Mean to You, Today's Professional?

Since the beginning of history, free enterprise has traditionally dictated how societies would compete for jobs, but now there is another dimension. It is this *empowered* workforce that is, in part, fueling the new work movement. From this perspective, value is not only derived from completing the work but also from the benefits the workers receive. Flexibility and empowerment for workers now rank higher than monetary compensation in overall job satisfaction, and smart employers are learning how to make that empowerment part of their corporate DNA.

Freelance personnel are willing to modify their compensation structures to match overall drivers of satisfaction. Now, the compensation construct has changed from wages and benefits, to a total compensation snapshot that includes quality of life. Next generation compensation structures now create a new way of thinking about work based on a free market system. This lends itself well to the trend toward fractionalization.

Kimmie Heard has been a Working Solutions agent since 2006. After working in technical support for Hewlett-Packard for many years, she decided her real future lay in being a virtualpreneur.

"I don't want to go back to corporate America again; it's not the right environment for growth, and I think the old system is dying," she says. "As a virtualpreneur, I can create my own schedule which allows me to be available to my family while being compensated well for what I do."

She notes that managing her time can be challenging, but feels the rewards have made that effort worthwhile. One surprising reward has been a high level of socialization with other WSOL agents.

"I worked the third shift at HP and had very little contact with fellow workers. Now I'm meeting other agents and they're actually helping me come out of my shell. I'll NEVER go back to the cube," she says.

The Next-Generation Motivation Models

Typically, people work through most of their adult years. This is what we are taught at a young age and what we generally plan to do until retirement. Presently, most professionals know that—for better or worse—permanent job security is a thing of the past. It is, in part, the absence of security that has shifted workers' mindsets over the last decade. This resulted in our economic preferences changing from work for the security a corporation could provide, to work on our own terms. This freedom is what drives and motivates the new, global workforce with no boundaries.

According to the crowdsourced reference tool Wikipedia, employment is the contract between two parties where, in return for compensation, the employee contributes labor and expertise to an endeavor of an employer and is usually hired to perform specific duties, which in turn are packaged into a job. While this definition of employment is still accurate, the concept of "employees" has changed.

The dot-com bust, followed by the terrorist attacks of September 11, 2001, forced many to question their priorities. Some professionals realized they were working for people they didn't care for, performing jobs they didn't enjoy, and chasing a sense of security that had all but slipped away. Over the last decade, those same professionals decided they wanted more control over their future. As a result, their economic preference changed from *security* to ***freedom***.

When this happened, the seeds that have grown into the New World of Work were planted. ***Today's workers are increasingly loyal to the skills they can monetize, not the companies they work for.***

The people in this new workforce are motivated by the freedom to work from where they want, and with whom they want. They ultimately realize they can make just as much money working for themselves as they can in the corporate structure. The Internet also enables them to learn anything online. Someone who is truly motivated can learn the skills required to be successful with the click of a mouse, and depending on the discipline get immediate feedback from social media sites,

Behance, GitHub, Pinterest and others. They know that their own ability and drive will enable them to write their own success story in this new world. —Mike Merrill, Chairman, Social Media Club of Dallas @MikeDMerrill

Over the last decade, this shift toward freedom created a freelance workforce that dictates how their knowledge and skills will be packaged and sold. As technology further enabled their freedom, they've been able to jump from the cube to the cloud in order to leverage virtual employment opportunities. In the process, they've learned to market themselves to the highest bidder (on their own terms) and work at the time of their choosing.

So, it's not just the unavailability of employment that is creating the New World of Work. Worker motivation has changed and more professionals are choosing to take control of their destinies. Freedom is the new currency for this workforce, while the old world clings to deceptively "secure" wages and benefits.

At Working Solutions, an original pioneer of the work-at-home virtual model, we initiated a research study on our home agents' social and economic preference functions. We concluded that the new contingent workforce:

- *Ranks flexibility and choice **above** monetary compensation*
- *Are **motivated** more by recognition and praise than money*
- *If empowered, are **more** likely to stay with their organization*
- *Receive **higher** customer satisfaction and loyalty scores than their brick-and-mortar peers*
- *Actually state they have an **increase** in engagement with their colleagues in a virtual environment*
- *Feel they are **more** productive in a virtual environment*
- *Demonstrated adaptability and willingness to change above brick-and-mortar counterparts*

This study reinforced the Working Solutions business model centered on a culture that believed skilled help wants to control their own destiny, so we designed a virtual work platform around these preferences. The goal was to empower, not manage, a virtual contract workforce. As a result of this fundamental cultural empowerment, Working Solutions continues to thrive. The company saw the virtual work movement before it became obvious, and understands the fundamental truth of the Virtualpreneur: Desired work is about creating empowerment and freedom, not security.

But worker motivation is only one part of the machine. As we mentioned, there are three drivers that create a three hundred-sixty-degree connection between the fractionalization of work and virtualization of careers. They are:

1) A global talent pool motivated by quality-of-life factors

2) A global talent pool that leverages productive technology to demand high-quality work at decent wages

3) A new work marketplace that creates value by breaking work into smaller units (fractionalization) and leverages supply and demand

The marketplace had to experience dramatic shifts and technology needed to rip apart boundaries to ultimately enable people to demand empowerment. *All of these factors* collided at once, which in turn, enabled the fractionalization of work.

To understand the new universe, one must grasp that virtual workers' **motivation** has changed. The originators of virtual work platforms like Working Solutions and Elance understood from the beginning that the old corporate carrot-and-stick motivation models would not be effective with the new empowered workforce.

In fact, some would contend that the carrot-and-stick model of motivation—where there is a promise of reward and a threat of punishment—never really worked because employees just found more effective ways to avoid responsibility. Regardless, the old-school tactic is completely ineffective with the current workforce.

Younger people especially are demanding more freedom in the workplace; there is no place for a nine-to-five schedule in their lives. Smart employers will give them the tools and flexibility they need to succeed personally and professionally, knowing team members will reward them with their best work. —Jeffrey Puritt, President of TELUS International

Unlike previous generations, who dreamed of joining a company directly out of high school or college and staying until retirement, today's operatives are **absolutely certain** that their current employer will not be their last. In fact, according to the Bureau of Labor Statistics, the average worker in the U.S. only stays at a given job for just over four years (data from August 2012). This suggests that whatever reward is promised must be tied to short-term objectives. As for the stick, threats of punishment are not as effective if an employee is in the mindset of moving on.

This situation results in a workforce with little or no loyalty, as well as virtually no sense of commitment to building the enterprise. Remember we mentioned earlier, today's worker is loyal to the skills he can monetize, not the employer.

What Happened to the Clock?

Adapting to the new environment and the empowered workforce will be a critical requirement for businesses to be competitive. If a company's leaders fail to recognize, embrace and prepare their managers for it, they will be left behind.

The next generation of professionals is wired differently and has different priorities. Young people have no use for the inefficiency of a commute or the limitations of the cube. Culturally, they were born into a virtual world and instinctively know how to maximize virtual collaboration tools to be effective virtually. If companies want to remain relevant to this next generation of talent, they will have to build a strategy that includes virtual work. —Tammy Valdez, Senior Vice President, LifeLock

Gone are the days of militaristic management styles dictated by control and intimidation. How do executives manage motivation in a virtual environment? Simply put, tie rewards directly to employees' intrinsic motivations—their sense of empowerment and enjoyment.

As an employer, you should prepare your management team to embrace the empowered workforce by focusing more on the passions of the worker, rather than the management of work.

Here are some tips for focusing more on the passions of the new worker:

- Ask yourself what the traits are for identifying management talent in your business. Virtual managers need to possess the ability to identify and interact with individual mentors for leadership, management and knowledge guidance.
- Identify the right individual with the right skill-set, experience and knowledge, and then establish clear objectives to be met.
- Manage and reward the results, production and outcomes, **not the time put into the work**. Self-motivated success of the freelance workforce is the new reward for efficiency, productivity and quality.
- Consider what management should look for in the empowered worker.

The key to managing this new workforce is to focus on their motivations and their passion for their work, rather than the time spent doing the work.

How to Recognize an Empowered Worker

Empowered workers universally share several attributes, which enable the fractionalized, virtual quality of the New World of Work. They are:

1) **Self-starting**: They have the ability to self-motivate and accomplish the task or achieve the objective.

2) **Educated**: They've gained critical knowledge, in either school, trade or by developing street smarts.

3) Technologically Savvy: They have the ability to navigate through today's connected world.

4) Committed: They are survivors who will not stop until they achieve success.

5) Connected: They are part of a team or network, or willing to join one.

In the NWOW, the bar has been raised. Skilled help no longer needs to live within a fifty-mile radius of your company, which means companies have the nation or the world as their recruiting pool. To the smart corporation, that translates into an ability to attract and retain the best talent from *around the globe.*

But even with no boundaries, there will be a shortage of skilled, knowledgeable prospects, and the best talent will go not only to the highest bidder, but to the best platforms for empowered work. These will be organizations that truly understand this new fractionalized, virtualized workforce, and focus on inspiring and motivating, rather than managing and legislating.

The number of skilled performance-based workers will grow at an unprecedented rate because of the globalization and fractionalization of work.

Remember, it is not only about compensation; other intangible benefits are at play. More importantly, educating managers to identify talent and embrace the virtual workforce is a requirement for managing the new talent pool of empowered workers.

Equipping Small Businesses to Compete for Talent

If you own a small business, the new work environment spells good news for you, but you must understand the natural laws of the new world. While it's true that the fundamental strength of our economic future rests in the hands of entrepreneurs and small businesses across the nation, it is imperative that small business leaders learn how to design a virtual talent strategy to maximize the fractionalization of work. This will ensure small business productivity and efficiency as costs are managed variably during growth spurts. Companies like Elance and oDesk understand this and have revolutionized the virtual work platform by offering free training to their clients on how to maximize virtual talent. They understand that for the fractionalization of work to take root, the playing fields must be leveled.

Frequently, small businesses are hampered by the absence of a scalable talent strategy. They ask themselves questions like: "Where will we find talent? Who will be qualified? How can I afford the talent I need?" These are the questions that keep most small business leaders awake at night. On one hand, they know they need talent to compete. But on the other hand, they are afraid to make mistakes or incur the expense of securing the best talent.

> *A virtual workforce is a great benefit to a small-to-medium-sized business like ours. About 70% of our workforce is virtual, which means we can recruit from a much larger talent pool. While we're based in Chicago, our people live in lots of different communities. So we get the best talent and they get to work from wherever they call home.* —*Jeff Furst, President and CEO of FurstPerson*

Stimulating the businesses that make up a substantial part of our economy means it will be even more important to fuel the new contingent workforce by encouraging a system of risks and rewards. By nurturing the innovation of this workforce and treating them as entrepreneurs, we thus can share the notion of risk and reward, which is the basis of entrepreneurship. If this is accomplished, we will accelerate the adoption of the New World of Work model.

The 5 "M" Strategies for Managing a Virtual Team

There are as many ways to motivate a virtual team as there are teams. However, we have identified five important strategies for managing a virtual team. These are:

1) **Model**: Set and communicate the objectives so everyone understands the objectives.

2) **Methods**: Obtain the right technologies and define the processes and methodologies for success.

3) **Metrics**: Develop the right objectives for task-related processes and functions that can be completed on time.

4) **Measure**: Monitor the performance to ensure the quality and performance.

5) **Motivate**: Find the passion for the individual, and remember that teamwork is key. Look for opportunities to socialize, interact and set the culture.

So, what do you want to do today? Where will you work from today? Whether you work at the office, car, home, hotel, pool, beach, relative's house, airport or restaurant, the New World of Work is the most efficient, flexible and productive environment in the history and evolution of work.

Regardless of your choice of profession, the new geography provides unlimited options for rethinking careers, all because the fractionalization of work and the power of convergence removed the boundaries. Without boundaries, new competitive models are free to evolve. For new models to evolve, technology must continue to enable the workforce, increasing its productivity and access to knowledge and information. To grasp the productive power of the new workforce, in the next chapter let's look at several companies enabling the virtual workforce, and thus providing fuel for the empowerment fire.

CHAPTER

6

CREATING A PRODUCTIVE, TECH-ENABLED WORKFORCE

A **SIMPLE GLANCE** around the subway station, coffee shop or restaurant illustrates the societal influence technology has had on our world. In locations around the globe, people sit gazing at their smart phone, iPad or laptop. They check emails, text friends, use social networks or watch YouTube videos and consume goods/services from web-enabled devices. For better or worse, we are all connected wirelessly.

> *There is a cultural shift underpinning this new workforce. The next generation of workers is naturally mobile and technology enabled. They are more comfortable online than they are in cubes, and are well suited for virtual work.* —*Jim Milton, CEO of SoundBite Communications*

These technological advances have certainly propelled the transformation and evolution of the workforce and workplace. The members of

Generation Y have grown up in a digital world, immersed in technology in every aspect of their lives. Work, play and all time in-between have equally converged, as our days are increasingly filled with multi-channel, digital or virtual worlds that have become the real world.

In 2012, International Data Corporation estimated that there would be 686 million smart phones sold worldwide and more than two billion users connected via networks of high-speed access. Since life has dramatically changed with the digital revolution, it is a natural progression that the way the world works will also change with a completely wired, digital workforce. So these statistics beg the question, how do we keep our virtual workforce productive?

Digitally Wired Recruits that Produce

Several factors enabled the virtual workforce and radically improved productivity in the process. According to Forrester Research, "The growth of consumer broadband Internet (56% of U.S. households have broadband today, up from 10% in 2002) has enabled more employees to work from home." In fact, according to WorldatWork, "a not-for-profit organization providing education, conferences and research focused on global human resource issues, over the last five years the number of telecommuters in the U.S. has risen by 43%."

Forester further adds, "As companies streamline workforces to focus on what differentiates them, they must outsource large chunks of work. And that means they must form deep partnerships with suppliers, partners, and customers while conducting work in distributed teams."

On many levels, the virtual call center was the first influential factor that led the work movement back toward distributed teams. It was followed by software development, then project management, then administrative work, and soon even knowledge-based work moved into the cloud, which positioned work to be accessed remotely.

Again, this movement was driven by both workers' demands for freedom and customers' demands for better service experiences from corporations. Customer service truly drove the enablement of cloud-based work because customers can demand a premium service experience at a fraction of the cost. As companies like Amazon and Zappos began to chart a new course in the definition of a superior customer service experience, other companies followed suit once they figured out how to get their workers productive and engaged.

Most companies understand that in today's customer-centric, social-media enabled world, they must compete by delivering a higher quality customer experience from their happy and productive staff, rather than focusing solely on the cost of their service enterprise. In our business, we see firsthand how forward-thinking executives that understand engaged, empowered workers actually improve customer experience. The residual effect is also obvious: Companies who deliver the best-branded customer experience will also control the market share in their industry.

Times Have Changed, for the Better

In the late 1980s IBM built a 500,000+ square-foot office park in Westchester, NY to house thousands of employees. It was a place where the personnel would commute to work, park their cars in massive parking lots and assume their eight-to-five jobs in their cubes—thousands and thousands of cubes.

Then, in 2009, IBM started to shift meetings to a new, virtual meeting place called Second Life. Second Life users can work, socialize and participate individually or together in groups in literally all aspects of the real world. These capabilities gave IBM the power to shift meetings and work to a virtual office complex.

Today the IBM Westchester office complex is a ghost town. It's an empty shell reminding us of the old Industrial-Age organizations of days gone by and the old office park.

Now digital office complexes allow organizations to work anywhere and still be connected to the team, rather than being isolated at home and away from peers and colleagues. Today's workforce can work anywhere at any time, while maintaining productivity from homes, cars, hotels and anywhere they have connected access, but now in the *real* world.

The New World of Work has answered the question:

How do you use whatever you have, wherever you are, whenever you want to do what you want to do? —*Francoise Legoues, Innovative Initiatives, IBM*

New social networks are not only for personal use. In an effort to keep employees engaged and happy, businesses are embracing them at a faster rate than the adoption of any previous technology since the personal computer. In fact, a recent survey by Manta, an online small-business community, shows that 90% of small businesses now use some form of social media.

The evolution of technology and connected social networks has reversed the feeling of alienation or loneliness when working remotely, bringing to mind John Donne's quote from 1624, "No man is an island." Virtual workers do not thrive when isolated from others; they want to be connected.

What does all this mean in terms of the skills you, as a new professional, must now bring to the global talent table?

Next-Generation Work Product

The number of skills required for specific work products has increased, and the digital revolution has created a connected network of knowledgeable employees capable of working wherever and whenever they want, as long as they complete tasks or achieve desired outcomes and results. And as expected, this flexibility leads to increased productivity. As noted, fractionalization results when routine work is broken down into smaller units or tasks. As this increasingly occurs among businesses around the globe, companies will hire fewer full-time employees and outsource routine jobs as contract projects.

Intelligent Workload Distribution

New software routing engines now enable companies to take advantage of a skilled virtual workforce by optimizing the business work streams or transactions and route to the individual best suited to complete. Genesys, the leader in customer-experience technology enablement, has created Intelligent Workload Distribution (iWD), which takes customer service delivery beyond the contact center by tracking, prioritizing and routing tasks to help companies meet customer demands and improve efficiency.

By prioritizing the work tasks and routing to the best people suited to handle the transaction and task, work product can be routed and distributed in a virtual environment to the most qualified, skilled individual.

Intelligent Workload Distribution enables enterprise-wide customer service delivery, provides greater business efficiencies and improves customer service by enabling users to quickly define priorities and service levels in real time—based on the business value of each task.

By optimizing the business work streams and enabling service delivery outside the contact center, workload management software takes the effort out of the customer service experience by ensuring that the right person does the right work at the right time, to meet customer expectations.

When you combine powerful software routing engines in the cloud that can fractionalize work product, with a global workforce of specialized agents, you are maximizing the potential benefits and efficiency gains of the NWOW model.

Success in the new workplace is about making silos disappear. Companies need systems that push work to people with the right skill sets based on business priorities, regardless of where they sit in the organization. That means organizations need to understand skills, and how they overlap, for everyone—contact center, back office, branches and the corporate headquarters staff. When this occurs, the efficiency gains are huge.
—Brad Baumunk, Workforce Optimization Lead, Genesys

Technology Is the Game Changer

As CEOs of companies and managers of workforces of talented professionals, we have witnessed up-close-and-personal the changing face of the New World of

Work. We see this book as our chance to pass on what we've learned about navigating through this new territory—which we believe houses the most important economic transformation of our lifetime.

This new paradigm is the most important economic change we've seen in our generation.

As you contemplate navigating the New World of Work, there are four key things to consider:

1) How to grasp the ever-changing landscape of technology

2) How to close the talent gap in your business

3) How to rethink your own personal career strategy

4) And, the power of the WHY

Technology has now enabled the worker in ways that revolutionize entire industries. Talent, skills, experience and knowledge can now be monetized anywhere in the world. Virtualization has become a game changer in the world of IT for every business, and it is laying the groundwork for the New World of Work evolution. Since IT has recognized the benefits of efficiencies and capabilities never possible in the brick-and-mortar facility, the marriage of virtualization and the contingent workforce is now complete.

The Number One benefit of Information Technology is that it empowers people to do what they want to do. It lets people be creative. It lets people be productive. It lets people learn things they didn't think they could learn before, and so in a sense it is all about potential. —Steve Ballmer, CEO, Microsoft Corporation

---

As technology continues to evolve, computers will provide increasingly automated tasks, leaving the more complex, dynamic-thinking tasks to humans. This will require a more qualified, skilled, and knowledgeable workforce than ever before. Just as the Industrial Revolution automated the manufacturing industry, creating specialized machine operators, the Knowledge Revolution will require specialized skill sets to complete the tasks and run the *technology machines* of the future.

As an employer, in order to compete for talent, you must have the best technology and tools for your workforce. More important than ever before, your tools must be able to integrate with other tools with minimal effort. Gone are the days when everyone ran proprietary software; now all applications need to have the ability to integrate and work together based on standards: a communication and transaction network where everyone and everything is fully connected and working together, virtually.

What are the required technologies for the future of work?

- High-speed access
- Minimum computing configuration (back to the mainframe)
- Collaboration (communication tools)
- Cloud-based applications (virtualization, grid networks)
- Mobile (ties them all together)

High-Speed Access

Broadband or high-speed Internet access is probably the single most important contributing factor to virtualization and the global workforce. It literally connects the world within milliseconds so people like you can collaborate and communicate in real-time, regardless of where you are located.

AT&T Chief Executive Officer Randall Stephenson commented on the need for more connectivity saying, "Fully one-third of all Americans don't subscribe to high-speed Internet access at all." AT&T is "trying to find a broadband solution that is economically viable to get out to rural America, and we're not finding one, to be quite candid."

How will America be able to compete for global talent if one of the key technologies, high-speed access, is not a focus of federal and state legislators? We need a renewed spotlight on the advantages of leading the world in technology innovation and improving high-speed access for everyone if we are going to compete in the race for high-speed connectivity.

We're now seeing the intersection of physical and virtual work worlds, driven by generational, societal, and technological changes. Add globalization to the mix and there's an increased need for significantly improved workforce collaboration to drive innovation. Dan Fallon, Former CTO Navistar and Board Co-Chair School of Applied Technology, Illinois Institute of Technology

---

Minimum Computing Configuration

In present companies, computers are the workhorses of all departments, connecting the personnel, assisting with work creation and completion, and providing information anytime, anywhere. The same is true in a virtual environment, where operatives connect to grid computers, mainframes or the cloud.

In a virtualized world with a global workforce, thin clients, which are making a comeback following their heyday in the 1970s, allow staff to tap into the computing power they need to work effectively. These simplified computers, which rely heavily on other, more complex devices in a network, now make it easier to secure, manage and scale workers from an IT perspective. IT departments are welcoming the thin-client and cloud technology with open arms as it becomes the next alternative to personal computers.

Collaboration

Collaboration is the new medium for information exchange in the cloud, and now, more than ever, technological advances in collaboration are driving a virtual, global economy. The next-generation workforce will require virtual collaboration skills to participate in group or team projects. Their individual contributions can be used independently or packaged together and reassembled as part of a group or team effort.

Collaboration and communication tools can now take the place of face-to-face meetings, phone calls and even email. These tools are dramatically different than they were a decade ago, and now they are a staple in every office environment, whether physical or virtual. Webcasts, web-conferencing and webinars have opened the door for a decentralized workforce that can work from anywhere.

The Cloud

Cloud computing is not the revolution; it is the evolution of what started almost twenty years ago, and now start-up organizations are relying on the cloud for unimaginable amounts of computing power, without any capital expense. Imagine being able to process hundreds of millions or billions of knowledge scans or searches without owning any technology infrastructure.

You can hardly look at an IT strategy document today without seeing mention of cloud computing, even though it has been around for years. So why all the attention? The model has now crossed the chasm to penetrate corporate America, which traditionally relied on internal infrastructure. This is a significant shift in IT mindset in what will certainly be remembered as a disruptive technology strategy that changed the way the world works, literally.

Mobile

We would not do the book justice without focusing on mobile devices. Smart phones and tablets are changing the world at a greater pace than the adoption of any technology prior to their existence. Connected to high-speed access and the cloud, they are fast becoming the standard for staying connected in a virtual world.

Remember we mentioned that anyone with a smart phone can change the way they work? You now have the tools to monetize your value, your skills or your experience in a virtual environment.

Want to hear a staggering statistic? The Futurist Society predicted that by the end of 2012 there would be more smart phones on the planet than humans! One step further, by 2016 there could be ten billion smart phone users or 1.4 mobile devices for every human on the planet.

Understand how the cloud and mobile devices are changing the way we live, and you will recognize how the New World of Work will empower the worker and change the way the world works.

The New Auto Assembly Line

What happened when Henry Ford changed the way automobiles were manufactured? His ingenious business model, which included paying his help wages that allowed them to purchase these horseless carriages, created built-in customers to buy his automobiles. This turned Ford's laborers into satisfied new customers, forever changing the way the world of commerce operates.

Technology is the key to creating the new assembly line in today's workplace. Virtual work platforms that remove all boundaries between the type of work offered and the type of work accepted is the key to ensuring we don't try to over-manage virtual talent and thereby kill the very spirit of it.

Think about what happens when companies compete for talent. Basically, in a no-boundaries world, the worker literally punches into work they find satisfying as long as the compensation is commensurate with the value of their output. The worker is empowered, and technology enables more freedom by ensuring the **work** is managed, rather than the person. This type of thinking, which is aided by technology rather than management, will increase the fractionalization of work, and thereby increase the pool of talent.

We noticed the move towards a boundary-less world over the last decade. In the beginning, it was only something large companies could afford. Today, finding the best talent globally is becoming as common as searching for a highly recommended restaurant online. Today, it's clearly more efficient for companies to hire talent online, regardless of their location.
—Alex George, Chief Technology Officer, Astute Solutions

Just Google It

There is no better example of how to succeed in the New World of Work than Google. The legend of how Larry Page and Sergey Brin invented an entire industry based on searching the Internet has become entrepreneurial lore.

Google processes more than one billion search requests each day and consistently boasts the highest number of visitors of any website in the world. What Google unknowingly created was technology-enabled access to information that continues to power the new work machine.

Those companies that pioneer new ways of empowering virtual workers will win, while professionals who find their passions and market them in the New World of Work will ultimately rule. To take full advantage of the fractionalization of work, be prepared to try new ways of working and new ways of being.

As more and more companies adopt similar models and expand their labor reach globally, the cascading effect will become an accelerant for every organization to embrace the model or face irrelevance and extinction. The empowered will challenge the status quo of yesterday's organization and raise the bar on performance, creating frightening competition for organizations that fail to adapt.

What Does the Future Hold?

First, the world has no boundaries and everything is global. Anyone or any company with value to offer can market goods or services anywhere in the world with a click of a mouse or on a mobile device. Individuals can contribute using collaboration tools. Today's networks provide the horsepower to enable group-work and crowdsourcing. Seamless communication across all channels, combined with the virtualization of most forward-thinking teams, creates an entire new organizational model.

In the New World of Work, we like to think of this as the next organizational hierarchy, and it exhibits powerful contrasts: Technology

is changing so rapidly that it is increasing the efficiency of all organizations, while empowering customers as noted in Chapter Four.
Customers are very different today than they were just a decade ago:
They are more informed; they learn, live, work and play differently,
aided by new technology.

While business is changing with technology, it's important to remember
that your customer looks very different today and is being changed by
the same Information Revolution. In the next chapter, we'll show you
how to capitalize on the needs of the new customer.

CHAPTER

7

THE CUSTOMER SERVICE REVOLUTION

To truly understand the origins of virtual work, customer service must be explored. Customers are constantly evolving and are increasingly more demanding. It was, in part, because of their demands that virtual customer service was born.

Fractionalized Work Serves the Customer

The best part of the fractionalization of work is that it aligns a business' motivation, enhanced customer service, and the empowered workforce's ability to *compete for work* on the basis of its ability to provide exemplary customer service. Think about that for a second: As a business executive, you can combine fractionalized work with a virtual workforce that can compete and work toward the same objectives that make companies more competitive. Fractionalized work in this new world is the ultimate way to build a service legacy that a business can leverage.

Presently, technology is enabling new service models. Understanding the new customer in a multi-channel world requires all companies to rethink customer service. Purchase decisions are now made with an abundance of information available on the product or service, as well as the reputation of the company and its attitude on how it treats the customer.

In early commerce, purchase decisions were made on the convincing presentations of the salesmen. Later, radio and television permitted companies to build brand equity through media outlets with advertising campaigns so powerful they could overcome product deficiencies or shortcomings. Do you remember the early television shows and commercials in the 1950s and 1960s when customers were comfortable with their purchase decisions simply because everything was brought to them by some large company? Next came product placements in movies and sitcoms.

Today, social media and the exchange of information are so instantaneous consumers have a plethora of real-time, detailed opinions and customer feedback on any product or service. If the product or service does not live up to the claims or expectations, the entire world knows— in real time.

A competitive focus on the customer is now required to secure, retain and build customer lists. Today's customer has high expectations and demands skilled, experienced and knowledgeable support through any channel they decide to use to reach your company. This means that your customer service must be available 24/7/365, through any channel (voice, email, chat, text or social media) that your customer chooses to use.

To give them that, businesses need to tap into a talent pool that is ***motivated*** by their passion for service and their willingness to be the best servants. That's part of the New World of Work!

Embracing the Multi-Channel, Connected World

Many companies are inundated with technological enhancements to ensure they are competitive in the new multi-channel, customer-centric world. Some simply stick their heads in the sand, while others are leapfrogging ahead. Instead of worrying about the effects of a multi-channel, connected world, why not embrace it?

What does that mean to you as a businessperson?

Forward-thinking executives understand that the newly empowered customer will control the market share over the next decade. ***Customer service has become the central nervous system of the new wave of e-commerce companies.*** What is the ultimate expression of complete customer satisfaction? First-contact resolution and knowledgeable representatives who are empowered to make decisions. Together they define the ultimate expression of customer service.

At reInvention we are committed to giving employees whatever they need to succeed, whenever they need it. That means they'll always have the right tools, including the most up-to-date technology in the industry, along with consistent management support and the freedom to use their skill and know-how to make on-the-spot decisions. We understand that they are qualified professionals and trust them to make decisions that will serve the best interests of our customers and the whole reInvention community. —Hugh Davis, Co-founder of Market Research Firm reInvention

---

What defines the culture of tomorrow's corporate leaders? Customer centricity, entrepreneurial spirit, innovation and tapping into the new empowered workforce. There are a number of very successful, early adapters to this customer model. No doubt, you likely use some or all of them every week. These innovative companies have cracked the code of customer service in the NWOW.

Pay attention to this word-of-warning: There have been hundreds of studies over the years that found interactions from customers with negative or uninformed employees would drive customers to your competitors; so the reverse will work to your advantage. If you embrace the requirement and demand customer service in today's multi-channel, connected, seamless world, you can grow market share and retain customers for life.

How do you deliver on customer expectations? By tapping into the passion, skills and knowledge of the workforce, and creating engaged workers. Secure engaged workers and empower them to make decisions, and you will build market share and keep customers.

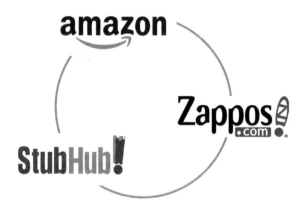

The most interesting research on Internet commerce was a study conducted by several Fortune 200 companies who once thought self-service was the path to save expenses and increase profits. The conclusion: Having customers serve themselves on the Internet resulted in a reduced average order value of 5-15%. Why? Because an engaged, trained, dynamically thinking agent representing your product or service will ask the right questions, educate, inform and ultimately sell more product. Now, product or service knowledge workers can represent your brand and improve your conversion rate, top line revenue and bottom line profit. By the way, they can work anywhere in the world as long as they are educated, experienced and trained.

David Litman, co-founder and CEO of Getaroom, has proven that he understands the customer better than most executives and as such is a great role model for our examination of the NWOW. Litman is a pioneer in the online travel industry, having co-founded Hotel Reservations Network, which later became Hotels.com. As CEO of Hotels.com, he was responsible for building the world's largest hotel e-commerce website from start-up to the final sale to Expedia.

Prior to co-founding Hotels.com in 1991 with friend Robert Diener, Litman was an attorney who decided that he would rather be an entrepreneur. Changing occupations and professions is also part and parcel of the New World of Work. Wanting to cater to his entrepreneurial spirit, he started a discount airline business in 1984 that became a multi-million-dollar wholesale airfare consolidation operation. In 1991, Diener and Litman saw the untapped potential in the hotel industry, and with an investment of only $1,200, the two founded what became Hotels. com. They sold their interest and left the company in 2004. Then, in 2008, they started Getaroom, a new hotel booking website focusing on handpicked hotel deals in major cities. True to their form, it has become extremely successful, too.

Driving the Customer Conversation

Genesys, one of the world's leading providers of customer service and contact-center software is uniquely positioned to help companies bring their people, insights and customer channels together to effectively drive today's customer conversations. Its goal is to turn customer interactions over multiple channels and time into continuous conversations that bring opportunity and value to businesses while building customer loyalty.

We are all tired of starting over at square one by providing the same customer information we provided in the Interactive Voice Response or to a prior agent every time we reach out to customer service or sales personnel. Have you ever lost your Internet connection as you moved to the final stages of checking out on an e-commerce retail site, only to find when you call the toll-free number you have to start over…again?

Genesys Conversation Manager is the latest innovation in the NWOW for providing a consistent experience across all channels. Now multiple channels and touch points can turn into seamless customer conversations. More importantly, anyone, anywhere in the world can help support the transaction or interaction. Now, there is a highly integrated routing engine and approach to uniformly handling all interactions and transactions.

Fractionalized, Virtualized Work Is the Secret to the Service Revolution

The late founder of Walmart, Sam Walton, was ahead of his time in many ways, especially in his commitment to customer service. He was fond of saying, "The goal of the company is to have customer service that is not just the best but legendary." In the new marketplace, this type of attention to customer service isn't just important, it's a matter of life or death for companies competing for the customer's share-of-wallet.

At Office Depot, we think about our business from an omni-channel perspective, and this approach has caused us to increase our focus on customer service relative to our e-commerce strategy. We asked ourselves, 'How would our store personnel respond if a customer was searching for a product and couldn't find it?' From that point of view, we engineered both reactive and proactive customer service responses for our web-based customers. This is critical because no matter how good your web experience is, some customers will always require human intervention as a means to best serve their needs.

Strategically, we found that as more customers moved their purchases to the web, it created the need for a different type of human service experience. It's clear that transactions can best be served by the web, but smart brands know that human interaction is an important way to differentiate themselves while providing a satisfying and memorable customer service experience. —Tim McGrath, Vice President, Customer Service, Office Depot

---

Today, customers enact commerce without driving to big brick-and-mortar facilities such as Walmart. Instead, they can shop while sitting at home or having a cup of coffee at Starbucks. The "always-on-and-always-open" commerce world has arrived and become the foundation for the next generation. In fact, it is all young people have ever known.

The Internet has created the multi-channel, digital world where everything from goods to services is a mouse-click or mobile device away.

What does this mean to you and to the companies who want to compete in the New World of Work? For one thing: you *must* adapt to the new demands of the next-generation, empowered customer. To do that, you have to adapt the way you think about the next-generation worker.

This entire chapter was designed to make one critical point: Empowered customers will respond best to empowered workers. Tap into the motivations of virtual workers who want to compete for *your* business, and you will tap into the nirvana once imagined in business fairy tales: laborers, who compete for the work you offer, will ensure that they take care of your crown jewels. They will, in turn, equip you to compete for your customer. This is the best part of the New World of Work. The brightest, most talented virtual workers will compete for work they enjoy. So you need to make the work something they enjoy and pay them for performance, which taps into their motivation. Then they will want to compete for your business, by ensuring that your customers are loyal to your business. That's the promise of the future.

And this competition for talented labor will open new worlds of opportunity for skilled professionals.

0101101010010100101010101010101010101010101011101 0101
0101010100110101010101101011101001101010010101010101
0010011010000101010101010101010100010010101101011 00
1101101010101010101010100010110101001010010101010
10110101010101010111010101010101010010011010101010110
101010010110101000101010101010100011010100010101010101
01010101001101010110100101011010101010010010101001010

SECTION 3

CAREERS: VIRTUALIZED

CHAPTER

8

TOMORROW'S CAREERS

CHINESE PHILOSOPHER CONFUCIUS insightfully noted, *"If you choose a job you love, you will never have to work a day in your life."*

This belief is at the heart of professionals charting career paths in the new business environment. Their motto could be: *"Do what you love, because nothing else matters."*

Fractionalization has undoubtedly changed the world of work. Fractionalization is, in part, being driven by the changing motivations of the labor force that demand quality of life as part of their compensation mix. And of course, as already discussed, technology enablement is continuously reshaping what work can be performed virtually. As more and more virtual work platforms emerge, traditional functions will ultimately move into the cloud. This has, and will continue to, reshape careers.

As a result of the massive distributional shift in the way we work, career-planning strategies must be completely overhauled. Forget asking your kids if they want to be doctors, lawyers or teachers. That language will soon be obsolete, as more careers take on virtual characteristics and are ultimately reborn. We are already seeing the effects of virtual instruction, which reshapes the notion of what a teaching career looks like.

And, with access to platforms such as LegalZoom.com, the majority of lower-level legal transactions can be performed virtually. What does that mean for paralegals and entry-level attorneys? It means a traditional job, in a traditional law office, could soon be a thing of the past. As for physicians' careers, doctors are already able to perform some diagnostic functions in the cloud. How will that change their career trajectory?

Tomorrow's career alternatives will become radically different over the next decade. In the old world of work, most professionals attended college and then chose a career. Although jobs may have changed over time, one's general career track usually stayed in the same hemisphere. An accountant typically stayed in accounting and engineers usually remained in R&D or operations. For the most part, we navigated within a general field-of-study from college through retirement.

Not anymore. Yesterday's jobs don't exist, today's jobs *won't exist* in a few years and tomorrow's careers haven't even been created. Face it: We need a new methodology for career planning.

There's also something else affecting occupational strategies: Even the jobs that currently exist within a corporation are becoming more difficult to categorize. For example, where will the social media department report to in the future? And should social media be centralized in its own department? The same is true with customer service. Should customer service even be a department or should it be embedded into every fiber of the corporate structure as Zappos does?

Corporate Walls Are Imploding

An interesting aspect of the New World of Work and the virtualization of careers is that by taking away the boundaries of work, corporate organizational structures are indirectly affected. In company after company, the walls are imploding as the old way of organizing work disintegrates, without the boundaries that once held them firmly in place.

With convergence and the onslaught of cloud-based computing disintegrating the boundaries of work, career lines are simultaneously being blurred. Companies now need professionals that are BOTH specialized and have a wide range of expertise. They need operationally minded marketers and sales-driven engineers. As the corporate walls implode, so do the boundaries of careers.

For example: One of the biggest battles being waged in today's corporations is the battle for the customer. In this social/digitally connected world, who handles social-media-based customer service—the comments, interactions and complaints?

Should it be handled by the customer service department? They used to take calls, but now their "conversations" are literally transparent on the social web. One bad service experience can be catapulted into cyberspace through Twitter and Facebook. Customer service has traditionally been managed by the operations function, yet suddenly marketing wants to control customer interactions to ensure a better brand experience. Marketers tend to be great communicators and can position things well, but they aren't used to working within the operationally centric customer service organization with its metrics and process efficiencies.

Public Relations professionals should probably handle the issues that percolate through social media. They are certainly more adept at handling sensitive issues, but they, too, aren't used to speaking to an onslaught of customers.

The truth is, companies will not survive unless the hard-and-fast walls built around key functions start to come down, beginning with customer service. As a result of a convergence-driven need for truly cross-functional customer engagement, companies are struggling with finding the right talent to ensure their brands are received well in the transparent world of social media. Consequently, this is creating a revolutionary shift in hiring and outsourcing strategies, and it's happening at light speed. As a result, new workforce models and technology platforms are emerging overnight. And, because work no longer has to be performed *at* the corporation, companies are free to think differently about workforce solutions.

Better yet, professionals are able to think differently about their careers. The new environment is opening a new dialog about the concept of a job, which will ultimately open the door to new career strategies. Just as in everything else in the New World of Work, there will soon be no boundaries to careers, whether that career is inside the corporation or wrapped in the cloud.

New Thoughts on the Meaning of a Career

There are two critical forces that are reshaping career planning strategies:

The Virtualpreneur Career: As discussed, new crowdsourcing or virtual work platforms match professionals' passions for the types of work they ENJOY, with companies who wish to contract with them for various projects. This is rapidly shaping up to be one of the biggest income-replacement trends in the global economy. We coined a new term for these people: Virtualpreneurs™.

Legislative Alignment: The biggest barrier to growth in the New World of Work in the U.S. is legislation. The manner in which jobs are classified in some legislation and the restrictions on the use of contractors versus employees will not allow America to be competitive in the New World of Work. (Look for a more complete discussion of this important career force in Chapter 10.)

The Virtualpreneur Career

Although projections differ, one thing is clear—The New World of Work has ushered in a new career option: the virtualpreneur. For professionals confident enough in their own ability, and desiring freedom and empowerment, almost any career today can be reinvented through the lens of a virtualpreneur.

Although work-from-home positions have been growing since 2000, they are now accelerating at a much more rapid pace. As of 2004, the U.S. Bureau of Labor Statistics claimed that about twenty-one million laborers, or 15% of the workforce, usually did some work at home as part of their primary job. In 2011, that number had mushroomed to twenty-eight million, an increase of 12% in the previous five years. And recently, the number of self-employed people has increased at a dramatic rate. According to Intuit's September 2012 Small Business Employment Index, nearly 600,000 people have gone into business for themselves in the previous eleven months. Put it all together and you have an unmistakably upward trend. In fact, the number of work-from-home positions is expected to far outpace traditional employment job growth in the next five years.

The majority of these positions are managerial, professional and sales roles; all jobs with more autonomy to begin with. As previously discussed, there will be significant deviations in home-based work models, facilitated by technological change, as empowered workers look for quality-of-life, rather than long commutes and tiny cubes.

This movement opens the door for a new career option combining the benefit of virtual work with the continued expansion of available contract projects. *Forbes* estimates that 32% of all positions are now part-time or contract-based. A survey from The McKinsey Global Institute finds that in the next five years, more than half of employers (58%) expect to hire more temporary, part-time and contract help for a variety of duties.

The combination of technological change and workforce globalization is propelling firms toward a virtualization model. Add to this the need for flexible staffing models that contract help offers, and presto, the virtualpreneur is born.

Rand Corporation, a well-known think tank, calls this a trend toward the "vertical disintegration of the firm." In other words, companies are shedding functions through outsourcing (and now crowdsourcing) in order to focus on specialized areas that define their core competencies. This is what we referred to earlier in the book as work fractionalization, or the break-up of traditional work roles into smaller, more specialized work units.

The forces driving the reorganization of work are simultaneously creating a shift toward nonstandard work arrangements such as self-employment and contract work. In this new work model, individuals compete in a global marketplace for project opportunities and work on multiple projects at a time. Teams continuously form, dissolve and reform as old projects are completed and new projects begin.

Some studies call this trend freelance, while others refer to it as micro-jobs. Regardless of the name, more positions are moving in this direction, and the U.S. Department of Labor estimates that millions of short-term recruits are needed. In most cases, these positions don't require that laborers be on-site, so they aren't tethered to the cube or required to work full-time.

The challenge is that most Americans don't even realize these jobs exist because of our century-old connection to the corporate job and the cube. Ironically, our smartest professionals are slowly finding the new gold rush of work—in the cloud. According to *Forbes* magazine, the percentage of U.S. workers with college degrees is at an all-time high, yet *only half of* **all** professionals age sixteen to twenty-nine have traditional jobs. One-by-one, as traditional work doors remain closed, professionals are opening their eyes to see that there is a brave new world and there are many more options available to them. This new fractional-virtual workforce model meets the needs of tomorrow's professionals.

A virtualpreneur career is a viable option for professionals who want flexible work outside of a traditional office setting. They can give up the commute, nix the boss, oust the nine-to-five workday and schedule work around their lives, rather than schedule their lives around the work.

The most important aspect of this trend toward the virtualpreneur is that it allows people to do WHAT THEY LOVE! As previously noted, jobs of the past featured rewards that were driven only on a time-based, output-based system. The best part about this new career option is that it recognizes professional passions and rewards those who get results.

Maureen Cutler became a Working Solutions agent in 2011, after her position as a medical bill coder was outsourced.

"I had worked for the same company for years, and suddenly was out of work at a time when there were no jobs. I had to take control of my life."

She loves the flexibility, convenience and lack of distraction. "I can be more productive in my quiet office at home. The best part is I've saved a fortune on travel expenses and business clothes. Now my commute is kitchen-to-office and I love it!" she says.

Maureen notes that, "The pay is awesome. You are in charge of how much you make. If you want to work fifteen or fifty hours you can; you have control over your income. It's fantastic."

She goes on to say that, even though there's little face-to-face contact between agents, there is a lot of socialization. There are chat rooms to communicate with other agents, and daily emails. And there's a great team of administrators and managers who keep us informed, motivated and recognize us for jobs well done." After just one year as a virtual-preneur, she says she would much rather work solo. "It's great; I never thought it could be so good. I would never want to go back to working for a large company. I want a long career with Working Solutions."

Virtualpreneur University

It is precisely because our university system has not yet caught up to the New World of Work that we, as the authors of this book, created a college-accredited Virtualpreneur University as a solution to the plaguing problem of an ill-prepared citizen base unrehearsed for the New World of Work.

We introduced Virtualpreneur University in January 2013 to tackle the problem of preparing the workforce to capitalize on this powerful career option. Virtualpreneur University includes college credits as a certificate program. It includes five modules, each with a different focus, but all designed to teach professionals how to navigate the New World of Work as virtualpreneurs. We also offer a significant discount for readers of this book to begin the journey towards a virtual career.

This book is meant to be a wake-up call and sound the alarm that there is a whole new way of working, and everything we knew about work is changing right before our eyes. We want readers to understand that, while our economy was fighting through the 2008 financial meltdown and subsequent recession, the boundaries to work have disappeared, seemingly overnight.

This book is also about how we can compete as individuals and as a society, and for jobs in the New World of Work. It's also about how companies can compete by finding the most qualified people, regardless of where they live. And it's about how professionals can compete by opening themselves up to the new environment.

It starts with understanding that the hottest new career today is that of a virtualpreneur. And we've dedicated the entire next chapter to this new career path. Taking the best of entrepreneurial DNA and coupling it with the new virtual work option, the virtualpreneur may be exactly what our country needs to restart its sluggish economy.

In the next chapter, let's look at how to capitalize on the new virtual career options. It's a bold new world and the virtualpreneurs are taking it by storm!

CHAPTER

9

CAPITALIZING ON VIRTUAL CAREERS

BUCKLE YOUR SEAT BELTS, FOLKS. Although you may not have heard about these professional options in the New World of Work, they exist.

A virtualpreneur career is a REAL opportunity for talented professionals to take their passion, as well as their skills, to the talent marketplace in a whole new way. Many are finding this type of employment more satisfying and, in some cases, more lucrative. Although the person who chooses to be a virtualpreneur must have the inner fortitude to deal with ambiguity, as well as the discipline to work with little or no supervision, if she chooses this path the rewards are exhilarating.

There are several business models that are proven for taking professional skills to market virtually, and many use a crowdsourcing model to drive success. These new virtual work platforms are revolutionizing the way work is done. They have eliminated the boundaries of work, and actively bring customers who want to hire talent to their platform, proactively.

Virtual work platforms are basically virtual employment offices that offer projects professionals can pick up and put down as needed. In some cases, prospects bid on jobs posted by hiring companies or they can post their own advertisement.

Virtual work platforms use *work-bidding* to match contract jobs with contract labor. This model is proving to be very effective. Let's look at how some companies are driving evolution of this new job-matching approach.

Change Your Perspective

There is one barrier that will keep many U.S. professionals from pursuing a virtualpreneur career. It is the access to traditional workplace benefits such as health insurance, life insurance, disability insurance and paid education, or training.

In a traditional employer/employee relationship, people expect these benefits as part of their compensation. The challenge is that these benefits have created a *dependency* on standard corporate work arrangements, and most U.S. laborers consequently ignore contract work because of the absence of health insurance. This is a mistake for several reasons.

Many, if not most, traditional companies have stopped offering any type of insurance benefits due to skyrocketing costs. In the United States, this crisis in healthcare coverage led to healthcare reform legislation that, if it remains in effect, mandates that individuals purchase health insurance and offers federally backed grants and other incentives for those who cannot afford the coverage. Some experts believe that this huge number of newly covered workers will reduce health insurance costs to a more manageable level. At this printing, the jury is still out on that issue.

Whatever happens in the political wrangling about affordable healthcare, the fact remains the same: These benefits will never be the same as they were twenty years ago. Companies can't afford to offer them. Therefore, the argument that a professional should take a traditional job for its benefits is flawed.

How to Succeed as a Virtualpreneur

Success means different things to different people. For virtualpreneurs, success typically means earning a competitive wage for work they enjoy and the freedom to do that work when, and from where, they choose.

Success as a virtualpreneur requires several attributes. However, the most accurate predictor of success as a virtualpreneur is the ability to shift one's mindset about work. This means letting go of the attachment to a set monthly income and corporate benefits. Most unemployed professionals overlook this career option because they are not granted company-sponsored benefits and there is no set income since the work is contract-based. Somehow, they perceive this as a lack of security, when in reality it is as secure as the old way of work. Consequently, most unemployed professionals spend months, if not years, looking for work in the old world, while virtual jobs go to citizens in other countries, because there are no boundaries in the New World of Work.

Being a virtualpreneur is a viable career option for professionals who want more control over their careers and desire more flexibility. It's also quickly becoming a powerful trend for companies to mitigate high overhead and rapidly changing workforce needs.

An Original Virtualpreneur - The Frugal Mom

Dawn Monroe, the force behind the popular blog, The Frugal Mom (www.thefrugalmom.net), started blogging in 2010 when her husband lost his job.

"At the time, my family needed me to find coupons to save our family money," she says. "I would find deals or free items, and my mom would call and ask where I found the deal. I'd hang up with her, and then my sisters would call. So, I started a blog and posted the deals and freebies I found to help them all. I never thought that two years later I'd have about fifteen thousand followers."

Dawn notes that working on her own schedule has allowed her to really "be present" for her children.

*"I set my own hours; I don't like to get on the computer when my chil-
dren are awake," she says. "I want my attention to be driven to them. If
I am sitting at my computer and tell my children 'one second' more than
once, then I close the laptop for an hour. My children are important and
I don't want them to think that Mom is always working. They come
first. With that said, I am not able to leave work at work. There is no
brick-and-mortar."*

*She adds that she sometimes misses getting away to work. "An office
environment would be somewhat more organized and quiet, but I would
not give up working from home and being in the presence of my children."*

*Based on her experience, Dawn advises potential virtualpreneurs, "Don't
give up. I started with three followers. They were my family members. I
remember the day I received my first blog comment. I thought, 'Someone
that I don't know is reading what I am writing.'"*

There are numerous careers that can easily be ported to a virtualpreneur
career model, and we expect that this list will continue to grow. They
include:

- **Teaching**: More and more classes are being offered online, and
  this trend is expected to increase.

- **Mystery Shoppers**: More than just liking a store, mystery shoppers evaluate an end-to-end brand experience from a customer
  perspective.

- **Customer Service Agents**: The backbone of the work-at-home
  sector is customer service agents, a job that is attractive to both
  young and old.

- **Virtual Assistants**: The once lucrative field of the administrative
  assistant has now been either eliminated or replaced by virtual
  assistants.

- **Writers**: Jobs for writers and editors are in abundance across the
  web. From newspaper blogging to book editing, there is no shortage of positions for effective writers looking to earn income.

- **Problem Solvers**: Businesses have a glut of problems and are frequently looking for professionals skilled at problem-identification and resolution.

- **Project Managers**: Always an important skill, virtual project managers are in hot demand globally.

- **IT Professionals**: Several virtual work platforms cater only to IT professionals and include traditional programming, as well as new programming languages to capitalize on the mobile application boom.

Todd Sullivan is a Working Solutions agent who has been with the company for five years. Now that he's able to work from his home office, he calls his old corporate life his "brick-and-mortar days."

"I'll never go back," he says. "My commute time is ten steps to the lower level in my house. I do have to work a little more to make the same income as in my brick-and-mortar job, but I can work from home, so it levels out if you think of the commute time saved, not to mention gas. The pros definitely outweigh the cons."

He advises anyone considering a virtual career to be sure they understand, "It's like any other job you would apply for; do your research, go online, and be sure you're dealing with a legitimate company. And make sure people understand you have a real job. And if you treat it that way yourself, you're sure to prosper."

How to Make a Virtualpreneur Career Successful

As more and more professions take on virtual characteristics, this career option will become a sought-after choice for the U.S. workforce, as well as around the globe. Although being a virtualpreneur is not for everyone, most professionals who are attracted to this model as a career option have the basic attributes that would ensure their success. There are four key traits that are necessary to make a virtualpreneur career successful. These include:

1) **Self-Motivation**: Virtualpreneurs don't have bosses telling them what, where and how to perform work. The more self-motivated the virtualpreneur, the more successful he or she will be.

2) **Prioritization Skills**: Since there will be multiple projects with a variety of deadlines, virtualpreneurs must be able to self-prioritize projects and manage client expectations.

3) **Resourcefulness**: Without the attachment to the corporate machine, resourcefulness is critical. Virtualpreneurs creatively use their social and technical skills to find tools, additional projects and unique solutions to work problems. Trial and error is part of the equation, and virtualpreneurs tend to be creative problem solvers.

4) **Basic Technical Skills**: Virtualpreneurs must be virtually connected and capable of managing their own personal computer and network connections. The good news is that there are virtual tools to assist in this task, and most computers have improved overall stability in the last decade.

Connie and Scott Sorensen are Working Solutions agents who found themselves out of work and in their early fifties. Scott worked as a mechanical engineer and Connie coordinated the openings of retail stores. Suddenly they were competing with college graduates for jobs that had been made almost non-existent thanks to the Great Recession. Then they joined the Working Solutions team.

"We didn't know this kind of opportunity was out there. It's been such a blessing," Connie says.

According to Scott, "We enjoy the freedom of being self-employed. It took a leap of faith to be self-employed, but we did not want to go back to cubicles. This position afforded us the perfect opportunity and freedom."

So, for professionals who want to capitalize on the New World of Work, the message is simple: Give up the cube and the commute, and look to the cloud. That's where the work and opportunities are. To capitalize on the New World of Work, follow your passions and think outside the box. Remember, there are no boundaries.

Finally, Let's Look at Some Compelling Reasons to Consider This Career:

Access: For starters, it's the most lucrative career option available to most professionals. Although, like any contract-based position, it takes time to build up a base of clients, the virtual work platforms make it much easier to find work than in other entrepreneurial endeavors. There are reasons for the success of oDesk and Elance: There is work! It's just no longer in the cube, and has moved into the cloud!

Work: McKinsey Global Institute, in its March 2012 report, *Help wanted: The future of work in advanced economies*, predicts that more than 50% of all work opportunities in the next five years will be contract. Although jobs are scarce, WORK IS NOT! Once you realize this point, it becomes clear that there has to be another way to capitalize on this New World of Work.

Market: More and more companies are looking to virtual freelancers to fill roles, especially during times of change and transition. It's clearly a growing market and the work is out there for you.

Now that you know the work is out there for you, you no longer need to fear the journey beyond the four walls of the corporation. In the next chapter, we'll explain why.

CHAPTER

10

NO BUILDINGS. NO FEAR.®

The New Way to Work

WAY BACK BEFORE THE TURN of the new millennium (which seems like eons ago), we saw that the world was changing. It was clear that technology would transform the way people worked.

In fact, working in a virtual environment is not new; it began in the early 1970s when technology first started to link offices together to the headquarters office. Known as telework or telecommuting back then, companies first started to realize the benefit of a virtual workforce almost fifty years ago. By decentralizing the workforce, people could work from anywhere, and, by leveraging technology, work could be joined together with applications and groupware.

So why did it take so long to understand the benefits? The main culprit was the employers' fear that they would lose control over the workforce. So why does working from someplace that is not a traditional office make some managers so uncomfortable? It has to do with our management need to see the recruits and what they do, a need for *control.*

Society also created a barrier from a psychological standpoint rooted in our human need for belonging and routine; it's the same reason people stay in a bad relationship or job: habit!

The reality is that the world has simply changed, and letting go of control is part of that. Even if you're a manager, you have to let go and let people do their jobs. —Jeanne Jones, Director of Consumer Affairs, ConAgra Foods

---

Beyond the Four Walls

Increasingly, companies are using freelancers to fulfill their needs, thereby enhancing flexibility so they can expand or shrink depending on demand. The new contingent workforce is laying the groundwork for the new virtual corporation that is no longer tied to the office building. The cost benefit allows employers to tap into an experienced, educated workforce-on-demand as needed—to support project work and seasonal growth spikes.

In order to fully leverage the new workforce, companies should address the advantages and disadvantages of why this new workforce is emerging.

Advantages

Employer	*Worker*
Flex staffing	Flexibility of hours
Reduced overhead	Work remotely
No benefits	Variable work
Scale	Variety
Improved margin	More opportunities
Specialty expertise as needed	Projects you choose
No labor unions	Less job discontent
Variable labor model	Self-employment

Disadvantages

Employer	*Worker*
No loyalty	Limited job security
Less retention	Minimal benefits
Lost domain knowledge	Cyclical wages
Challenging social aspects	Less career advancement

Even considering these disadvantages, the advantages are still tilting the scales to a new virtual contingent workforce, creating a mutually beneficial relationship between the employer and worker. And there is no longer a stigma attached to working in this capacity.

In the late 1990s, while working at GE TechTeam, a joint venture between General Electric and Tech Team, Tim saw the first signs of how the New World of Work model had evolved to the point of efficiency that could not be stopped.

GE TechTeam serviced large Fortune 100 companies for technical support and warranty management, focusing mostly on the call center trouble shooting and break-fix transactions associated with warranty support for the computer industry. Every fourth quarter, we would start hiring staff in October, knowing we would not need the support until after Thanksgiving, with the volumes peaking after Christmas until the end of the third week of January.

Since 60-70% of the support volume would come during that timeframe, a steady-state workforce was not needed year-round. The biggest challenge was recruiting staff for the peak periods, knowing the pink slips would be issued in late January.

Now, with the GE TechTeam example fresh in your mind, how does the new model look now? The benefits are undeniable; using the nation as your recruiting pool and targeted selection for recruiting the specialized skill set, a variable staffing model could have solved the challenges we had every fourth quarter.

Today, the cloud helps us deliver the same connectivity and productivity you would find in a brick-and-mortar office. The entrepreneurial spirit has surfaced and the new professionals earn respect for working for themselves in fields they are passionate about and on their own terms.

Legislation

Ironically, the New World of Work has nothing to do with national governments, because it was created by innovative entrepreneurs who saw a need to connect talent with companies who needed fractional/virtual workers, and they created platforms to make that happen. The challenge is that they inadvertently created a work movement so strong that it now threatens the corporate culture of our country.

And we in the U.S. aren't prepared. Culturally, we are conditioned to working in the cube, receiving praise for doing what we're told, being granted health benefits because we're inside the corporation and collecting a check every two weeks. The New World of Work is about results, performance and competing for work. In many cases, it's the antithesis of our old way of work distribution.

Counting Heads

Currently, the U.S. Bureau of Labor Statistics considers only jobs filled with traditional employees as part of the workforce. On its site, the agency refers to contract work as an "alternative employment arrangement." It defines the contingent worker as follows: "Contingent workers are persons who do not expect their jobs to last or who reported that their jobs are temporary."

Contingent workers do not have an implicit or explicit contract for ongoing employment. Alternative employment arrangements include persons employed as independent contractors, on-call workers, temporary help agency recruits and staff provided by contract firms.

In order to advance the model and progress, we must have legislation that supports a society and individuals who innovate and create.

New legislation should include classification systems that give contract workers their due by making them part of the American workforce. And laws should be enacted to bring contract workers under the protective umbrella of U.S. law.

As a publication from the National Employment Law Project, *Organizing for Workplace Equity: Model State Legislation for Nonstandard Workers*, notes, "Despite strong public support for nonstandard workers, the nation's employment laws have not kept pace with the growth in nonstandard work. Thus, nonstandard workers lack some of the most basic protections of labor and employment laws that apply to permanent, full-time employees."

The basis of the new workforce is that workers choose the "lifestyle" career because it meets their monetary and personal objectives, mainly freedom. Federal laws need to recognize the validity of this choice and count independent contractors and sole proprietorship businesses as part of job-growth statistics.

The old-school method for counting jobs is gone, or should be. We need to provide an environment and culture to foster the virtualpreneurial spirit of the new contingent workforce. Legislation needs to allow virtualprenuers to be counted as part of the employment numbers. Support for the independent business owner will help us create jobs, strengthen the economy and get us working again.

Time or Money?

Yahoo Finance and *Parade* magazine teamed up for a job satisfaction/happiness survey conducted in the second quarter of 2012 to discover how Americans view their careers, jobs, work environments and futures. One of the key findings in the Job Happiness poll was that more than 60% of Americans would go back and re-write their careers. Think about that for a second. Almost two-thirds of the people who make up the American workforce would hit the rewind button and start their careers over.

Why would the majority of working Americans want a re-do? This is an important question in the New World of Work because it leads to another critical question: How can we increase job satisfaction? The answer is to move the work to the cloud, fractionalize the work and develop a compensation-based structure for performance and quality. Hard work and creativity should be rewarded based on individual contribution and as part of a team working toward a common goal or objective.

The most disturbing statistic from the study is that more than 35% said they would fire their bosses. Is this because of the absence of managerial talent and leadership in today's business? Perhaps. But it does suggest that embarking on a self-directed, conscious career choice of working as a virtualprenuer in a career that you are passionate about will lead to increased economic output and job satisfaction.

Mercer Research conducted a study in late 2011, concluding that Millennial-generation employees (those born after 1982) are 50% more likely to leave their jobs because they do not believe they are in a "sound place to work." So, that means more than 50% the younger generation is looking for a better alternative.

The most compelling confirmation of the New World of Work model is that two out of every three Americans would like to improve their workspaces. These findings corroborate the need for the next-generation workforce that chooses the task/work product, sets the compensation structure based on a perfect market system and essentially works independently wherever they have access to the Internet. It also lays the groundwork for having world-class technology available for this workforce, which we will cover in Chapter 14.

Young people coming into the workplace are all about working with new technology and social media. They're comfortable with devices and don't need human contact in the same way older generations did. What they do need is flexibility. —Stephen Lynn, President and CEO, Dovetail Software

---

What does the contingent workforce feel is relevant to its well-being? The answer is job satisfaction, pure and simple. When you were in grammar school you were probably given very specific reasons why you needed to learn each subject and how the information would be applied in the future. Did all the knowledge you gained turn out to be useful or did it simply point you in the direction of a traditional career?

What happens when the rules change? What happens when you learn a different way or gain a specific knowledge that you are passionate about somewhere other than a traditional school? Can you begin to break through the confines of what society has dictated to you and allow yourself to create and innovate? Yes. All you need is a computer or mobile device and the Internet. Can you compete now? You bet you can.

Bottom line: The four walls that once kept people captive are gone. Over the last decade, technological and social changes have given rise to new, borderless business models. That means you, as a professional or business manager, have ultimate freedom. But here's the rub: You're now competing with a world full of other professionals.

Are you ready for this? Are you ready to *compete* for work? The global talent pool is ready, and they are not working in an office. Companies around the world are betting that Americans can't compete in a global talent marketplace without boundaries. Are you ready to prove them wrong?

Now that the world has opened up a global talent pool with no boundaries, what do you think will be next? What industries will benefit from virtualization?

0101101010010100101010101010101010101010101011010101
0101010100110101010101101011010011010100101010101010
0010011010000101010101010101010000100101011010101100
1101101010101010101010101001011010100101001010101010
1010101010101011010101010101001110101010101010100110
1011010011010100101010101010010011010000101010101010
01010101000011010101010100110111101010101010001010010

SECTION 4

TALENT: GLOBALIZED

NEW BUSINESS MODELS

IN MANY WAYS, the basic business model in a market-driven economy has not changed much in the past two hundred years. However, as everyone now knows, the Internet changes everything and the cloud has arrived to change the way we work. Business models that would be unsustainable without the "long tail" of the net can become enormously successful when a service or product can be sold to millions of new customers with little overhead, almost no advertising expenses and global distribution.

The trends of the New World of Work have already been responsible for making many men and women wealthy beyond their imaginations. The business models that supported this wealth have evolved only recently and continue to morph into different systems. How will industries be served? What is the next wave of businesses that will be launched using the new model?

An Evolution

At the end of the last century, the move to Internet-enabled business/working models had begun, with industries like IT and graphic design taking the lead. Now, as exponential technology growth dramatically increases capabilities, a growing list of industries is moving at least some functions into the remote arena.

Even sectors like healthcare and education, which once seemed bound by the walls of hospitals and classrooms, are seeing some functions move to the virtual world.

Crowdsourcing—A Force for the Future

The real distinction between traditional outsourcing and crowdsourcing is that the task or work is outsourced to the public at-large, rather than to paid employees or dedicated independent contractors.

In reference to the distributed work environment, the work can be fractionalized and assigned to the general public or to assembled communities for transaction completion, problem solving or production work models.

The model to distribute work to various groups based on specialization or experience is not new, but now the work is no longer confined within the four walls of a building. The Internet has enabled the true sense of crowdsourcing to exist globally, and the world is changing with its limitless boundaries.

Now someone can monetize his individual contribution based on work experience and education with just a mouse click, phone call or text from a mobile device. More importantly, when the contributions of others participating are bundled in a similar forum, fractionalized work output can create a competitive advantage similar to having an all-star team of pro athletes.

As well as embracing the virtual work model, businesses must create physical spaces that can easily integrate to the virtual world to drive productivity and innovation. —Dan Fallon, Former CTO Navistar and Board Co-Chair School of Applied Technology, Illinois Institute of Technology

Who wins in this new scenario? The company with the leadership and management team that can identify and recruit people with the right skill-set, assemble the tasks to be completed and deliver the results based on objectives.

There are many successful organizations that have already seized this competitive advantage. They include:

Crowdsource.com
Designcrowd.com
Chaordix.com
Elance.com
Support.com
oDesk.com
Workshifting.com
Mechanical Turk
Solutionary
Gigwalk
TaskRabbit

British Prime Minister Winston Churchill famously said, "Those who fail to learn from history are doomed to repeat it." Using history as our guide, we should be able to predict what will happen in the future. By applying the rapid changes of technological advances, we can start to "dream" about what the future of the world will look like in ten, twenty or thirty years.

One thing we know for sure is that the move toward virtual business models will continue, steadily building one global workforce.

The Home Agent Model

Working Solutions was one of the original pioneers of the home agent contact center model, leveraging a virtual workforce and technology to change the model. This model is now widely employed by businesses around the globe, providing businesses an ever-growing source of talent and giving talented individuals the option of monetizing their skills without ever leaving their homes.

Leveraging the remote worker allowed us to overcome the challenges presented from staffing limitations for dedicated, skilled help. The model has exploded beyond the contact center and now includes all transactions and interactions that can be fractionalized in the cloud.

Amazingly Ahead of the Curve

Online retailer Amazon has one of those business models that would not be sustainable in the old economy. However, in the New World of Work it is effective, because it creates a company with no boundaries. Amazon in many ways was the original pioneer of leveraging the dynamic in the retail space. Now it has divisions and initiatives dedicated to exploring the evolution of the model and the virtual platforms that have been built.

One such example is the Amazon Mechanical Turk (MTurk), a crowdsourcing Internet marketplace for work that enables computer programmers—known as "requesters"—to coordinate the use of human intelligence to perform tasks that computers are currently unable to do. The requesters are able to post *Human Intelligence Tasks* (HITs), such as choosing the best among several photographs of a storefront, writing product descriptions or identifying performers on music CDs. Workers, who are called "providers" in mechanical Turk's Terms of Service, can then browse among existing tasks and complete them for a monetary payment set by the requester.

The Mechanical Turk provides business access to an on-demand, scalable workforce; it is a glimpse of how work will be fractionalized and distributed in the future. The lesson is powerful: Technology now enables everyone to work everywhere and the MTurk is a proven example on how work will be fractionalized, packaged, delivered and completed.

The Numbers Don't Lie

Historians, futurists, political leaders and business leaders all hear the same story, and they believe in the evolution of the distributed workforce model. They agree that it will create an improved economic structure for both companies and personnel, making the model unstoppable.

Now, how can you, as a businessperson, benefit from what you believe will happen and what you now know about the New World of Work? First, fully commit to the model. Second, hire mangers who understand how to compete for talent in a virtual environment. Third, build a technology infrastructure in the cloud capable of supporting your business.

For me, the real WOW factor in the virtual model is the nimbleness/ flexibility it offers. For example, we did a program for a toll-free 800 company and were able to staff (using an at-home model) for their peak time, minute-by-minute because we had the staff ready and waiting! That kind of flexibility is a must in today's competitive global environment. —Paulo Silva, Vice President, Latin American, Xerox

---

Retooling Manufacturing

The near implosion of the automobile industry in the United States in 2010 hastened a trend that has been coming for many years: Old-style manufacturing is being retooled in a way that workers and their unions never thought possible. The basis for this reworking of the factory floor is the fractionalization of job tasks. The concept of "just-in-time inventory," which was a staple of planning in the automotive industry for decades, has been incorporated into the area of human resources.

The old way of staffing for manufacturing jobs has not been profitable for many years, but it took a near-collapse for the industry to realize that it must either change its way of doing business, or it would be out of business. While it has been painful—change always is—the automotive industry is slowly moving into the New World of Work.

In the old days, it was said that a service company's assets went up and down in the elevator each day. While today's talented workforce may never set foot in a company elevator, skilled, motivated contributors are more important than ever before.

3D Printing...The Next Transformative Technology

One of the biggest break-out technologies for the New World of Work is affordable, high-resolution 3D printers. Historically known as additive manufacturing, these three-dimensional printers mold objects out of wax or plastic, working from digital configuration provided by software. They have become the latest tool for professional creators, hobbyists and specialty manufacturers.

What was once a futuristic dream in science fiction is now an industrial strength reality that can be available in home offices like laser printers in the 1980s. Imagine the ability to create almost any shape, geometric object or feature by using a printer in your virtual office. You can even buy a color 3D printer for more accurate design features.

The technology is now more advanced and selling for as little as $1,000. The biggest prediction of this new disruptive technology is that it will drive an entirely new group of workers who can seize the means of design, rapid prototyping, fabrication and production from large corporations.

Now, additive manufacturing can take virtual blueprints from CAD designers all over the world and compile them into digital cross sections for the printer to use as a guideline to create a detailed 3D model of anything! If you now look at the manufacturing process as we know it, the 3D printer will not only revolutionize how we produce, but it will also fractionalize the work, created by a global workforce. Does the theme sound familiar?

Experts estimate it could become the next trillion-dollar industry. The big question is, will it become a jobless industry because it will simplify the design and manufacturing process, or will it create job growth? If you go back and look at the evolution of technology from an economic standpoint, new industries create jobs, but they are different.

History teaches us that the jobs created from this new industry will demand different skill sets, and a new group of entrepreneurs will drive economic and job growth through innovation and new business models.

If you want to find the best talent for jobs in one of the new industries being created, you have to understand how the NWOW works to your advantage. We'll show you how to make it work for you in the next chapter.

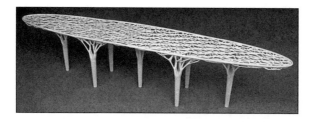

Trabecula Bench by FreedomOfCreation

Trabecula Bench was inspired by the inner side and low density part of a bird bone. The structure is very lightweight, but the 3-dimensional structure makes it still extremely strong. Trabecula is Latin for "small beam." The near 2-meter length of the bench makes it the biggest Laser Sintered piece from a 3D printer to date. Designed by Janne Kyttanen.

CHAPTER

12

COMPETING FOR
VIRTUAL TALENT

ANY HR EXECUTIVE OR SMALL BUSINESS OWNER has experienced the drowning sensation of being hit with a deluge of resumes. In the good old days, companies had to take the time to review (and hopefully confirm the accuracy of) resumes, at which point the best of the applicants were invited to come in for more formal interviews.

This process took a lot of time and was inaccurate about 50% of the time. So, how difficult will it be when these applicants are virtual? It will be even tougher to get the right person for the job. It will help, however, to have a game plan, and that's what this chapter is all about. Recruiting this new virtual talent will be the currency of the New World of Work.

The competition for virtual talent begs several questions:

- How will you identify talent?
- How will you train and manage them?
- Should there be hard metrics for results and outcomes?

- What are the standards that we use to measure the new contingent workforce?

To help in making these decisions, remember that there are three key characteristics that represent a successful virtual workforce. When contemplating hiring virtual help, these traits should be at the top of your list.

1) They should be skilled.

2) They must be flexible and adaptable.

3) They must be self-motivated.

Each of these traits is important on its own, and they become critical when combined. Let's take a look at each characteristic and why they are important in the new global marketplace.

Skilled Workers

Qualifications are critical. Finding those who are most qualified will be the most effective strategy for fractionalized work. People with experience, education, training and credentials will be able to compete in a virtual environment, marketing their specialization to the highest bidder. In many ways, this is a perfect market and the world has become the marketplace.

The process of identifying qualified people will require a new form or system of management. Managers must be able to identify the right skill set and design a results-based compensation structure to effectively leverage the virtual workforce. They must then direct specific work products to experienced recruits with proven performance and reputation for results. Think of this as a social-media approval rating for work performance. (Hopefully, there will be many more LIKES than LOLs!) These will be objectives-based compensation structures with clearly defined measurement tools.

Flexibility

Flexibility is the key to the talent acquisition in the new structure. If the key to motivating in the New World of Work is flexibility, our organizations must learn to embrace the value of flexibility in order to retain top talent.

The value of the worker is to complete the task and fulfill a need. If you are working for a company and you fulfill their needs, you are a valuable employee, regardless of when or where the work is completed. The sooner you understand and embrace the New World of Work, the sooner you will be at a competitive advantage.

Self-Motivation

What motivates the new workforce? As we discussed in Chapter Five, the new model of a virtual contingent workforce suggests that there are both intrinsic (internal) and extrinsic (external) motivation factors that influence the contributions of the new contingent workforce.

Intrinsic Motivation comes from the enjoyment and feeling from the actual contribution and completion of the work itself. The secondary result is the sense of belonging to the social network, group or community through individual participation and involvement.

Extrinsic Motivation includes the economic or monetary benefit of completing the work product or task. The form of currency will now take on a broader meaning, suggesting that there will be more than money motivating the new workforce. Social recognition is becoming a powerful extrinsic motivator, similar to social status of the past.

This new workforce places greater value on flexibility, individual contribution and control of one's own destiny to succeed in the New World of Work and the global economy. Companies that capitalize on the new currency of the contingent workforce will have a competitive advantage with a new labor-cost model.

According to John Slocum, SMU Emeritus Professor, Author of Demystifying Your Business Strategy, Routhledge, 2013, Professional Business Management Consultant, these are the key benefits to competing for virtual talent.

1) Businesses will save money by drawing upon a global workforce, usually at contractor rates. The publishing houses and the movie studios have been doing this for decades; we call it a "networking organization." They bring on specialized talent, complete the project and then move on to the next project with the next set of specialized people.

2) Integration is key; virtualization requires heavy project management and program integration to harness all the global talent. This model allows for contractors to use contractors, so the management has to be tighter than in a single business unit.

3) Companies want tailored resumes for their personnel needs, targeted selection for talent. It will be important for both the worker to index and company to be able to identify specialized skill sets; generic resumes in the cloud will not raise the bar on talent.

The Union Mindset Shift

Organized labor unions had their place in American history, especially in the early factories before federal legislation dictated hour limitations, work environments and safety requirements. The impact of the labor unions has led to labor-based political parties, an important constituency in some elections and certainly a factor when looking at how jobs are counted. However, the power and corruption of the unions has led to their reduced importance as a part of corporate America.

The empowered virtual workforce helps employers avoid unionization discussions, unless they are already addressed in previous labor agreements. Unions actually increase costs for both the employer and worker with their fees, rules, laws, bureaucracy, layers of management and legal negotiations. Avoiding *the need for* organized labor unions will help the New World of Work model gain momentum and grow.

The days of the massive conglomerate inundated with multiple labor unions are gone. Future workforces will dictate their own hours based on flexibility and, in the process, become more productive. Trusting in the outcome will enable even greater output. Workforce-development strategies for motivation, reward, recognition and incentives should incorporate the economic preference of the empowered workforce in order to thrive.

In late 2012 the world heard for the first time that a beloved brand was about to close its doors, in part due to failed union negotiations. Hostess Brands, a conglomerate mainstay of the Baby Boomer era of processed foods, announced that declining sales, coupled with unsuccessful union labor negotiations and repeated attempts to restructure, had failed to produce a successful business model. Hostess was left with no alternative but to sell its assets.

The Hostess story is interesting for many reasons. One could argue that its product line-up of predominantly unhealthy foods could be the culprit. Others have argued that management is to blame. But from the perspective of the New World of Work, the requirement for unionization must be evaluated as well. Will labor unions be relevant in the New World of Work? If work truly becomes a marketplace where the best pay goes to the best work, then unions will disappear as quickly as Twinkies and Ding Dongs.

Education and training of these newly empowered professionals and workers must also change in order to meet the demands of the New World of Work. Read on to see some of our suggestions for transforming education to better meet the needs of the new marketplace.

CHAPTER 13

EDUCATION MUST CHANGE

GLOBALIZATION IS NO LONGER ABOUT wicked corporate executives outsourcing jobs, or governmental policies favoring offshoring. In fact, it never really was about those things. Jobs are being crowdsourced on virtual work platforms regardless of what governments legislate or corporations create. There are no boundaries.

For the United States or any other nation to compete in this New World of Work, one long-standing institution much change. That institution is education.

To prepare professionals for this world will require a close look at education. America's colleges and universities are in the best position to assist American businesses and transform talent by equipping them with the skills to capitalize on the New World of Work—if they can meet the challenges of this new world.

How Education Can Help Renovate the Workforce

Three unique educational strategies are evolving specifically to address the challenge of renovating the workforce through education. These are:

1) **Strategy 1—Create Something New.** New virtual university models have been evolving since the University of Phoenix was created by Dr. John Sterling in 1976. Every year, more colleges using virtual formats are accredited. On the surface, it might seem like this is the answer. But is it?

2) **Strategy 2—Blow It Up and Start Over.** There are some leaders who think our entire post-secondary educational system is flawed. They point to Steve Jobs, Michael Dell and Mark Zuckerberg, wildly successful entrepreneurs who never graduated from college, yet were lifelong learners who created transformative products, companies and business models.

3) **Strategy 3—Build from What's Working.** Recently, major educational institutions have begun to experiment with new ideas that leverage their infrastructure, but are approaching the market differently.

   a) The much-hyped Empowered, a professional certificate program by UCLA, is like workforce training on steroids.

   b) Free online courses by world-class institutions? It's true and it's shaping up to be an educational incubator that may just save large university brands.

Strategy 1—Create Something New

Although the University of Phoenix got its start in the late 1970s, it did not hit consumers' radar screens until the dot-com era. For most, that was the period when all things Internet finally made sense. Since that time, numerous online universities have popped up, all promoting a more efficient and more cost-effective way to obtain a college degree.

The number of college students enrolled in at least one online course has been increasing for more than a decade, according to the Babson College Survey Research Group's annual survey of more than 2,500 colleges and universities. More than six million students took at least one online class during fall 2010—a 10.1% increase over the year before. An online class is defined in this survey as a course where more than 80% of all content is delivered online, and there are typically no face-to-face meetings with instructors.

The growth of online education far exceeds the growth of higher education overall. The total enrollment in universities and community colleges increased by nearly 120,000 students during fall 2010, a mere 0.6% increase over the previous year.

Online education has become a critical strategy for many colleges and universities, with 65.5% of all chief academic officers reporting in 2011 that "online education is critical to the long-term strategy" of an institution, up slightly from the previous year.

The quality of online courses has also continued its upward climb. Sixty-seven percent of academic professionals rated online education courses as the same or superior to face-to-face instruction, an increase from 57% in fall 2003, when this rating was first published.

However, the real challenge with migrating college curriculum to an online format is that it doesn't get to the root of the problem. Whereas online higher education made sense a decade ago, in the New World of Work, the college degree itself is now in question—not merely the delivery format.

Although the data is far from conclusive, it is no longer safe to say that college education assures a better employment picture. There are two fundamental reasons why this is so.

First, in the NWOW it's about matching the persona of the worker with the types of roles. College degrees are long on content and light on career strategies. To compete in the new marketplace, having a clear career strategy is paramount.

More importantly, new workers are intuitively self-educated and notoriously driven by a "learn as you go" culture fed by YouTube and Google. They don't want to learn *anything* they don't need to know (which is the basis of most collegiate systems), because they have confidence they will learn it, **when they need it.** This is based on their understanding that in the Information Revolution, knowledge is at their fingertips.

Strategy 2—Blow It Up and Start Over

Peter Thiel is a technology entrepreneur, investor and philanthropist. Ever heard of PayPal? Peter first gained attention in 1998 as co-founder and leader of this ground-breaking company, clearly an innovation in commerce.

Today he is known as the mentor of the PayPal mafia of entrepreneurs, as well as for his warnings of a lack of technological innovation, possibly with severe economic consequences. He works to accelerate innovation by identifying and funding promising technology ideas and by guiding successful companies to scale to dominate their industries. It's *how* he does it, however, that has the media and tech world buzzing.

Thiel created the 20 Under 20 Fellowship in an attempt to generate a wake-up call in response to business, government and educational apathy. He and others refer to our current educational system as the *Education Bubble* and point to its ineffectiveness at creating game-changing leaders.

A college education was once regarded as a first-class ticket to a better life. However, the rising costs of higher education, as well as the burden of student loans and a less-certain job market, have left many wondering: Is college really worth it?

Organizations like Thiel's have made many people wonder if a college education is for everyone. Should everyone take on massive student debt? In fact, total student loan debt has surpassed one trillion dollars, which is more than total credit card debt in America. And, unlike mortgage holders, students cannot declare bankruptcy to discharge their debts. Outside of repayment, only death and disability will eliminate the debt. Furthermore, since the cost of college has gone up 439% since 1982, and many argue the quality of learning has stagnated, the value of an education is now becoming a favorite media topic.

Peter believes that "excellence doesn't require a degree." Despite being well educated (Stanford undergraduate and Stanford law degree), Peter criticizes the collegiate system that has created a grand illusion that college is the only path to a happy, successful, intellectually stimulating, fulfilling life. He points to world-class leaders who lead game-changing businesses but don't have college degrees.

Thiel's Foundation launched the Thiel Fellowship, a two-year program in which twenty leaders under twenty years old each receive $100,000 and mentorship from a network of innovators, engineers, scientists, thought leaders and business development experts, in exchange for walking away from their college education. It's one of the most amazing experiments since the university system was created in the 1800s.

Thiel graduates have started several companies, secured book deals, raised million-dollar funding rounds, won international awards and sparked a do-it-yourself educational movement. The second class got underway in June 2012 when the next twenty fellows were awarded scholarships.

The Thiel Foundation notes that by no means are they telling all college students that they should drop out. But they are encouraging all students to think hard about the educational paths available to them. For many, going to college requires taking on tens of thousands of dollars in debt, yet the return on that investment is being tested by prolonged economic challenges.

It may take a few more years before the Thiel Fellowship gathers enough data to know whether or not this strategy will work, but one thing is clear: We're all watching. Thiel got our attention.

Another education pioneer of sorts is Professor Eddie Obeng from the United Kingdom. Professor Obeng is an original virtualpreneur who quit a high-paying job decades ago for the freedom of working on his own terms. In addition to choosing quality of life over traditional employment, he saw a frightening, but exhilarating trend, which he now calls World After Midnight, or WAM for short.

The basis of WAM is that in the Internet-enabled world, change is occurring faster than our ability to learn about it. In the old days, we learned about a new trend and thus were equipped to maximize it. In the new world, by the time we learn the change, our knowledge is obsolete. WAM's impact on education is powerful, as Professor Obeng explains:

"The World After Midnight breaks the model of traditional instruction because linear progression no longer works in a World After Midnight. Because the pace of change is so rapid, global networks and access to information trumps a linear focus on degree-seeking."

What is clear is that for professionals to compete in the New World of Work, something has to change about the way we educate our future workforce.

Strategy 3—Build from What Is Working

As more and more data pours in that highlights the very real weaknesses in our educational infrastructure, some colleges are thinking out of the box.

One veteran educator who is only too well aware of the need for an educational transformation in this country is Dr. Hasan Pirkul, dean of the Naveen Jindal School of Management at the University of Texas at Dallas.

"We are going to have to reinvent our approach to education to compete, just as U.S. professionals need to reinvent their approach to compete," he says. "We all know that education is the key to sustain our economic prosperity, but our leading universities have not created sufficient capacity in educational fields that are in high demand such as engineering, computer science, applied sciences and business, which leads to a knowledge gap (between what the new generation of workers need and the educational system is providing)."

He goes on to explain, "The challenge for American workers is that they have to be educated for high skill jobs as they cannot compete with the low wages of workers from the developing nations for low skill jobs."

According to Dean Pirkul, the country's educational system has had plenty of time to retool to effectively serve the new workforce. Unfortunately, however, our universities have been slow in making needed changes.

"Colleges saw the virtual work movement twenty years ago, but focused on instructional application versus business transformation," he says.

And that, he concludes, "has opened the door for for-profit entities to offer education and instructional solutions."

Two scenarios have emerged that will test the old monarchy of higher education posh and could potentially be well positioned to capitalize on the New World of Work boom. They each attack the problem from different perspectives. One suggests that a re-education of our current workforce is a priority and the other observes that it is affordable access to great thinking that trumps all.

The two perspectives have something in common: They are founded in the powerful belief that something has to change in the way we educate future leaders and it's better to experiment from inside the ivory towers than to have the system brought down by "villains" such as Thiel.

Re-Education of Workers

Professional certificates have become increasingly popular in the United States. In fact, certificates currently make up 22% of postsecondary credentials, compared to just 6% in 1980, according to a recent report by Georgetown University Center on Education and the Workforce. According to the Institute for College Access and Success, about 3% of the workforce—or four million workers—have certificates. The rise in professional certificates throughout the country is largely due to their significantly lower cost and shorter time commitment than a graduate degree. It's also an ideal way for college graduates and/or working professionals to get additional professional and practical training, improve or expand professional skills or explore alternate careers, while still working part- or full-time.

UCLA seems to understand that our workforce must be reeducated. And rather than publish a paper about it, they partnered with media personalities and put a stake in the ground by forming Empowered, an extension of UCLA and based on a professional certificate program.

Empowered is a unique combination of job-centric certificate programs designed for real-world employment needs, integrated with personalized career counseling. It could be an example of the old world meeting the new. UCLA is building on its strength of experience and connecting students with a community of peers and instructors through a unique iPad app. It has launched a massive media campaign with spokespersons from Hollywood, and designed a comprehensive program that lets professionals reinvent themselves, one certificate at a time.

What Empowered gets right is the *learn-as-you-go* culture that is the basis of the New World of Work. What is yet to be seen is if they chose content that fits the new paradigm. Current certificates range from Project Management to College Counseling to Marketing and Health Care Management.

This is an interesting assortment of certificate programs for older professionals caught in the valley between the old world of work, and the new. Their motto, "Turn past experience into new opportunity," strikes at the challenge workers face in this new world—how to capitalize on experience and find the opportunity.

Access to Great Thought

Many colleges have offered web-based courses for years, but top-tier research universities are adding a new twist in digital learning. From Harvard to Stanford, a growing number of world-class universities are taking the doors off to introduce the average person to the power of great thought. Renowned universities are now offering their most popular courses online for *free*, allowing anyone with an Internet connection to learn from world-renowned scholars and scientists.

Yes, we said free. Free.

This new approach is called Massive Open Online Courses, or MOOCs, and it has the potential to transform elite education at a time when colleges and universities are fighting an epic battle to remain relevant. Buried by reduced budgets, rising costs, diva professors and media outcry over soaring tuition and student debt, MOOCs may be both an experiment and a Superman cape.

From the outside looking in, MOOCs clearly lower instructional costs and expand access to higher education. At the present, students can't earn college credit for the courses, but that doesn't seem to matter to those hungry for learn-as-you-go insights from great thinkers. Having access to great thought is the basis of the New World of Work, and this new delivery model could fuel technological innovation and economic growth.

So, who's responsible for this revolution? Part of the answer is Coursera.

Coursera is a social entrepreneurship company that partners with the top universities in the world to offer courses online for anyone to take, for free. They envision a future where the top universities are educating not only thousands but millions of students. Their technology enables the best professors to teach tens or hundreds of thousands of students, giving everyone access to the world-class education that has so far been available only to a select few.

Another free online program is the Khan Academy, which is actually a nonprofit organization dedicated to providing free course and learning tools to students ranging from kindergarteners to older, returning students. The Academy says it is on a mission to change "education for the better by providing a free world-class education to anyone anywhere," and is on its way to creating a "global classroom."

The University of California Berkeley said it would start making online courses available this fall through edX, a competing Web portal launched in May 2012 by Harvard University and MIT with $60 million in funding from the two schools. EdX officials say 154,000 students from more than 160 countries registered for MIT's first online course, "Circuits and Electronics," this past spring. Only about 7,100 students passed the course, but that's still a lot more than can fit in a lecture hall.

As one might expect, the new online courses are attracting mostly older workers who want to upgrade their skills and knowledge, but may not have the time or money to attend classes on campus.

It's rumored that some schools may soon offer college credits for Coursera courses. If more schools follow suit, the online teaching could allow more students to attend college and graduate faster, experts say.

The real test is whether or not MOOCs generate revenue for top-notch universities. The belief is that companies such as Coursera can give universities access to a whole new demographic, and the free classes give professionals a chance to sample the university elite. Free trials and sampling of this kind have proven very successful for all sorts of companies.

The easy-to-administer courses typically feature short video lectures followed by quizzes that test students on the concepts they just learned. Most math and science exams are graded by computer, and in some cases students evaluate each other's assignments.

For the professional, MOOCs are at the heart of the New World of Work: learn as you go, gain access to great thought and think outside of the box.

Education must change, or it will die—at least as we know it now. Just as the workforce goes, so goes education. In the New World of Work, everything has changed, and it continues to change, right before our very eyes. Education must also keep pace with the light-speed pace of revolution underpinning the New World of Work. If there are no boundaries to work, we must rip the boundaries off education. Many of the strategies outlined in this chapter aim to do that.

Furthermore, these strategies are each based on an NWOW core value: "Collaboration is the new currency." Collaboration is the critical core value that takes opportunity and turns it into enterprise in the new business landscape.

We believe that the educational system of the future will be a combination of practical, career-based programs designed to help the labor force thrive in the new world, along with university programs for those more inclined toward a traditional college education.

All of this ultimately leads to a newly empowered workforce. Successful companies will learn how to attract and retain these new people. We'll show you what we mean in the next chapter.

01011010100101001010101010101010101010101011101010101
01010101001101010101010110101101001101010010101010101
00100110100000101010101010101010101001001010110101100
11011010101010101010101010100010110101001010010101010
10101010101010101010111010101010101010101001101010101010110
101101010010101010101010101001001001000000010010101010101

SECTION 5

NOW WHAT?

CHAPTER

14

CLOSE THE TALENT GAP

THE ULTIMATE EMPOWERMENT OF TOMORROW'S WORKFORCE is the power of the *free*lance worker. The engaged, empowered worker is passionate about her vocation and actively seeks training, knowledge and skills to compete on her own terms. The speed of change for businesses looking for new skills is fueling a new approach to how they respond to labor shortages for the specialized jobs that they need to fill.

Transform the Learning Experience

As noted in Chapter 13, traditional education focuses on preparing an individual for a future career. Schools are building facilities, adding faculty and increasing costs for the students. One solution to the problem of how to train the new knowledge worker is certification programs businesses manage themselves. This eliminates the economic barrier that traditionally holds back students with little or no economic means, allowing them to complete the curriculum. Participants who complete the programs will then have valuable work experience, knowledge and training at their disposal to do with as they wish.

Working Solutions was unable to find a university-based curriculum to support the needs of its virtual contract-labor workforce, so it created its own curriculum and launched Virtualpreneur University. Since collaboration is the new currency, Working Solutions partnered with Succeed on Purpose to develop the curriculum and learning management system, and launched the program in January of 2013.

How do you position yourself or your firm to take advantage of the virtual workforce? Identifying the talent with the right skills and investing in knowledge development will create a competitive advantage. Companies that embrace the model can then hire highly specialized people on a part-time basis, as opposed to incurring the expense of full-time employees.

Where Are the Workers?

According to labor statistics for 2012 in the *World Factbook*, there are more than two hundred million people unemployed globally. However, as noted earlier, more than one-third of corporations and businesses worldwide are looking to hire the right talent for specific knowledge or human-task jobs. Thus, there exists a dilemma: There is a significant gap between the skills, experience and education required, and the availability of these positions in a global economy.

What does that mean to employers? When specific talent is a scarce resource and at a premium, we must expand our boundaries to include the global workforce who can work from anywhere, virtually.

The most competitive companies are learning how to attract, hire and retain the best talent—the most experienced and knowledgeable workers for the positions required. The key to success in the new world is this: *flexibility!*

New-World-of-Work employees will work on their own terms, and they require a work/life balance as well as the ability to work remotely. The largest part of compensation is now based on flexibility, and the most competitive companies will master the art of creating a mobile workforce that can work from anywhere.

Teleworking and flexible organizations are now creating an opportunity to attract and retain the most qualified talent, allowing them to work from alternative worksites. Virtual service management platforms can create a work flexibility arrangement to allow staff to perform and complete assignments at alternative locations.

Identifying the right knowledge worker is the key to the future success of business, regardless of where the worker resides. Creative CEOs want their teams to cut costs while adding flexibility for those with specialized skill sets. In order to accomplish that, new-age companies must learn how to engage the virtual workforce.

Creating a variable cost model to support labor requirements will enable an on-demand labor force, improving margins for companies. Transferring fixed labor costs to variable costs will allow companies to reward skilled people more for productivity, performance and efficiency.

The best labor, the top performers, will ultimately demand more compensation in the marketplace, because they can deliver results. The new cost model will support the change in economics. There is also a need to organize the work differently.

Organizing the Work

The virtualization of work requires IT systems that can support the skilled workforce. Companies must identify the people who possess the skills needed to support the work and the key management functions in any organization. The three key areas for organizing the work output are:

1) **Systems.** Back and front office technology infrastructures are required to capitalize on the virtual worker. Innovative and intuitive applications that facilitate effective and efficient work interactions and transactions will drive results in a virtual environment. Collaboration tools for individuals to share ideas will create innovation and efficiency. But more importantly, they will foster the psychological benefit of being part of a team. Companies should never underestimate the *purpose* component of manag-

ing and measuring talent and insuring their systems, processes and organization are aligned to deliver on the promise.

2) **Talent.** We continue to reference "talent" in this book and we do so very deliberately. The New World of Work is all about access to talent. The ability to find the right individual with the right skill set for the right job is the reason the model will create market opportunities for the skilled worker who can compete in the virtual world. Embracing new cloud-based platforms, social media applications and collaboration tools will allow individual workers to compete beyond the constraints of their previous four-walls employer. Convincing forward-thinking executives to focus on the output rather than the internal vs. external resources will allow the educated, experienced, skilled worker to break down the barriers to attracting talent.

In order to be able to compete, workers have to identify their own SWOT (strengths, weaknesses, opportunities and threats) in the same way any business would. Statistically, individuals who understand their SWOTs are open to learning additional skills. Obviously, it's easier to teach someone interested in learning than it is to convince someone who isn't sure why he or she needs to do so.

Emerging jobs do not look like the same ones our grandparents and parents once had. They require a different set of skills. Automation has stripped off the routine, simple tasks, leaving a more complex interaction. Recruiting efforts for these jobs has shifted to an inspired sole proprietor with the tools to surpass the competition because they have the skills and tools to deliver results.

The General Manager of Major League Baseball's Oakland Athletics, Billy Beane, adopted a talent-evaluation program that is taken right out of the New World of Work playbook. In the book *Moneyball*, author Michael Lewis covers how the team, led by Beane, changed the way professional baseball players are chosen and compensated.

The book focuses on the team's analytical, evidence-based, saber metric (technical analysis of baseball) approach to assembling a competitive baseball team, despite Oakland's disadvantaged revenue situation. Using this new talent evaluation approach, the Athletics became a team that contended for the American League pennant, while keeping its budget balanced.

3) **Measurement.** New initiatives and measurement metrics will be needed to help design and build the organizational structures to support the virtual workforce. Empowering the new workforce actually *improves* results. When trust is incorporated into the employer/worker relationship, the emphasis becomes accomplishing the tasks and achieving results and outcomes. The focus will change and results will follow.

In order for a virtual model to be successful, you have to trust employees out of the gate. It's like sending your children off to college; you have to trust that they'll make the right decisions and be successful. —Jeanne Jones, Director of Consumer Affairs, ConAgra Foods

---

When an engaged workforce specifically targeted for the job and armed with the tools to be successful is unleashed, you have a recipe for success. By bringing in highly skilled labor for flex-capacity or short-term assignments you will be able to use variable cost labor models to increase output and margins.

If flexibility is crucial for successful companies in the new marketplace, what does that mean for the workers? What happens when you find yourself unemployed and realize that, no matter how skilled or what level of experience you have, the job has gone away and it's never coming back?

Regardless of your employment status, if you're reading this book, you must understand that this new world is here, and it's changing everything we knew about work. The new landscape calls for a complete rethinking of your own career strategy.

We've designed a powerful career-planning tool to assist you in making this leap. Think of it as a blueprint for the New World of Work!

CHAPTER

15

RETHINK
CAREER STRATEGIES

FOR PROFESSIONALS NAVIGATING THE NEW WORLD OF WORK, the journey can seem overwhelming and frightening. Although it's certainly a different frontier, moving from the cube to the cloud should not be frightening. The New World of Work is ripe with opportunity for those professionals who understand how to map new career strategies.

Carl Pascale spent twenty-two lucrative years with Lockheed Martin before being jettisoned in one of several corporate layoff rounds. Carl thought finding another job would be easy. However, after nearly ten months of searching and countless workshops and seminars from so-called experts, Carl had nothing. He was bewildered.

In the summer of 2012, he asked a question that struck fear in his heart: "How can so many people be following such good advice on their job search and not be getting results? Is it possible that these experts could be wrong, and that maybe the career marketplace has changed?" The question changed his entire focus. Shortly after his fated self-imposed question, Carl heard Terri Maxwell speak on the Talent Market Shift (the basis for parts of this book), and started the process of waking up.

"The old way isn't working. There are talented professionals in the marketplace, but they can't seem to find any open doors because they are looking for the jobs that they lost. But they no longer exist! Now that I understand the new world of work I'm not going back. I don't know where this road will lead, but I know that I want to be part of building something that makes a difference. My advice to those on this search is that you have to let go of what you knew about the talent marketplace to find open doors."

A Quick Review

Let's recap a few critical points from previous chapters.

First, the New World of Work is based on three revolutionary workforce trends:

1) **Work has been fractionalized**—Routine projects have been broken into small units and grouped together. What that means is that many former "cube" jobs no longer exist, because they have been fractionalized and placed in the cloud.

2) **Careers have been virtualized**—There are *no boundaries* in the New World of Work, and as a result, careers are now virtualized. What that means is that there is a lot of work in the cloud, but finding work (virtually or locally) requires a grasp of the impacts of the virtual-career landscape.

3) **Talent has been globalized**—Given the fractionalization of work and the virtualization of careers, companies can now source

talent globally. It's not about outsourcing, and it's not about our government. There are no boundaries to work, and most work can now be done just about anywhere. That means that talent can also be found ANYWHERE.

Secondly, jobs as we know them have changed. Today, work opportunities abound in primarily two areas:

1) **Virtualpreneur**: There are numerous work opportunities for virtual professionals who want to take their talents to market through a virtual work platform. However, most of these roles are, and will be, contract-based.

2) **Small Businesses (Under $100 Million in Revenue)**: The majority of positions, both full-time and contract, will come from small businesses, not large corporations. Smaller corporations don't hire the same way. Many things about finding a job in a small business are different than today's job searching strategies, and only a proactive small-business job search will yield results.

Most displaced workers were catapulted from larger corporations with revenues in excess of $1 billion. However, the majority of the job growth today is in small companies with revenues under $100 million. The challenge for most professionals is that small companies don't hire the same way large corporations do, and people don't know how to find this readily available employment.

Small businesses rarely advertise open positions, but instead prefer to fill them through referrals and networking. In many cases, small businesses are looking for professionals to fill roles, rather than employees to fill jobs, which means typical job postings are irrelevant or non-existent in most small businesses.

Finding Your Place in the New World of Work

Whether you're looking to become a virtualpreneur or are trying to find a job in the maze of the New World of Work, one thing is true: You need a new career strategy!

Making the Leap to a Virtualpreneur Career Strategy

For those of you seeking a career change, hopefully this book has encouraged you to think about becoming a virtualpreneur. For all of the reasons noted in this book, it is by far the hottest career trend of this decade. A secure, standard-paying job is an illusion in this economy, and a traditional employment relationship now offers only a pittance of economic security. Yet opportunities abound in both virtualpreneur and contract work, and even in small businesses.

The biggest leap professionals must make is to give up dependence on traditional workplace benefits and instead look for work opportunities of all kinds. New programs are popping up that outline benefit options for contract workers. The hard part, however, is giving up the perceived reliance on these once-secure corporate benefits.

The final leap to make is the actual structure of work. In most jobs, work is structured and ordered, managed and managed again. There are opportunities for career progression and regular oversight from managers. In the virtualpreneurial world, the individual is responsible for seeking projects and riding out periods of low demand. There is no well-defined career ladder, but the rewards of freedom and the ability to increase earnings based on performance far outweigh the limitations of this new system.

A virtualpreneur career is a great option for those who want structured work opportunities without the micro-management of a corporation. What are the two best reasons to give up the search for a job and seek a virtualpreneur option? They are **opportunity and freedom**.

So would you make a good virtualpreneur, or are your skills better suited for small businesses? Here is a powerful tool to help professionals develop a career strategy for the global marketplace.

Building a Career Strategy

The move towards careers being virtualized has ushered in a new way to think about career planning. Another factor driving career change is that most work opportunities are being created by small businesses, rather than large corporations. In the social/digital decade ahead of us, where technology changes in an instant, so too will the jobs. It's counter-productive to fight this powerful trend; it is more advisable to adjust to it. Instead of worrying about your job, build a new *career framework* and operate within it.

After working with professionals in varying stages of career transition, Succeed on Purpose created a career-planning system to prepare professionals for this New World of Work. The Succeed on Purpose Career Framework serves as a map to this new world and uses a series of decisions for career planning. It starts with three simple personas. (Personas are like identities.)

Decision 1: Your career strategy starts with Career Personas. Are you a doer, solver or builder? (See diagram next page.) We've outlined descriptions of each of the personas to assist you in this process. The material should also help business owners and talent executives find people with the right qualifications for given projects or positions.

Persona 1—The DOER: A DOER persona prefers a familiar environment and a predictable set of responsibilities. Although tasks might change, DOERs function best in a familiar structure. They are motivated by getting things done and by operating in the "known." They prefer structured work and the opportunity to get things done. DOERs tend to navigate to more routine functions: administration, operations, accounting and IT.

If you have a DOER persona, your career choices should focus on roles in corporations or small businesses where duties are somewhat predictable. If you elect a virtualpreneur path, look for stable contracts with a well-known Virtual Work Platform like those outlined in this book. Business owners and hiring executives should remember that DOERs prefer predictable work and are easily empowered by intrinsic self-motivation. Therefore, they make perfect additions to any team, project or company.

Persona 2—The SOLVER: A SOLVER persona is highly motivated to solve problems. SOLVER personas have a wide range of career choices in this new virtualized world. Whether they lead a team, work on a team or work alone, is irrelevant. Business owners and executives will find that they have a burning desire to solve problems and work best when given the freedom to do so.

Because most corporations typically "outsource" problem-solving assignments to boutique consulting firms or solopreneurs, those SOLVER professionals who are open to contingent work can easily replace their incomes doing contract consulting, virtually and locally. In fact, SOLVERS make great solopreneurs and virtualpreneurs.

Conversely, SOLVERS are also in demand in most companies that need analytical problem-solvers to address myriad challenges. Either way, SOLVERS have a variety of career options available to them, if they follow their core nature, solving.

Persona 3—The BUILDER: The BUILDER persona is a powerful force in smaller businesses, under $100 million in revenue, as well as start-ups. BUILDERS are never satisfied with the status quo; they *must* build something. And once it's built, they need to make it bigger or better, or move on to the next thing.

BUILDERS are tapped for difficult projects: building new departments, creating new methodologies or carving out new territories. They show up in every discipline, and can be uniquely identified by their drive to build something of value. They will change jobs every one to three years, even if it's with the same company.

Business owners and managers know that BUILDERS make great entrepreneurs and powerful leaders in companies of all sizes. However, they do not perform well in hierarchical corporate structures. BUILDERS excel in small businesses that are growth-oriented. BUILDERS invent, create, build, solve and serve in a variety of roles across all industries.

The key for a BUILDER persona isn't what they do, but *how* they do it. They must feel as if they are building something of value.

New World of Work Career Planning Strategy

Decision 1:

Career Persona	Doer	Solver	Builder

Decision 1: As you reflect on your career, don't think about traditional career tracks. Think about your persona. Which persona best describes you? Focus on the framework and target your job, career or business search using this framework. Once you've decided on your persona, advance to the second decision. How would you prefer to work?

Decision 2: Evaluate your Persona–Based Work Options. Does your persona fit a role working in a larger corporation (above $100 million) or a small business (under $100 million) or possibly a start-up, or should you evaluate virtual work platforms, start a business or franchise? (See diagram below.)

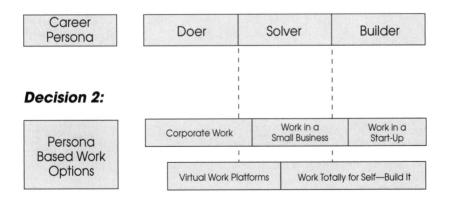

Decision 3: Based on whether or not your Career Persona is better suited for that of an entrepreneur or a role working for someone else, evaluate the categories of careers available to you.

Should you consider becoming a virtualpreneur and making your way on a virtual work platform such as ELance, oDesk or Working Solutions? Should you try to build a solopreneur business as a consultant, coach, trainer, etc.? There are many local solopreneur opportunities. Or should you start a business franchise, become an entrepreneur, or build a business based on something you enjoy?

If you're better suited for working for someone, consider the size of business. Each business segment has a need for something different, based on its evolutionary state (more on that later).

Decision 3:

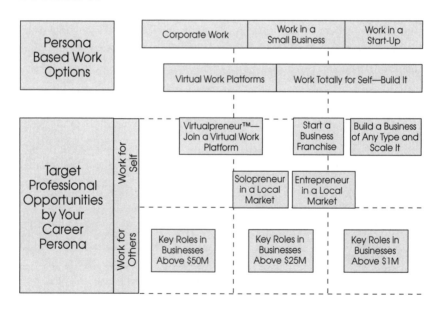

As part of your career strategy, knowing the size of the companies you want to work with (whether doing contract or role-based work) is critical. Companies take on different personalities based on their revenue size. Succeed on Purpose has prepared these charts to assist professionals in identifying the characteristics of a specific small business segment.

Characteristics of Small Business Segments

Micro Business or Start-up: Under $1 Million in Revenue
Much like an infant, start-ups are messy, and they change almost daily. They need a lot of care and feeding, and usually only Builders are suited for a start-up environment, and all of the builder roles (Change Agent, Team Builder, Execution Driver and Game Changer) are sought out by start-up executives looking to build their management teams. Risk is high and pay is usually low, however, there are tremendous rewards for those professionals who find a great start-up and stick it out during the ups and downs. Professionals who seek these opportunities must enjoy hard, creative work and enjoy a business environment that changes constantly.

Small Business:
$1 Million–$10 Million in Revenue

Small Businesses who have survived "the first million" and are up and running move on to this stage. Small businesses are a little more structured than start-ups, but can still change very rapidly depending on how fast they are growing. Think of them as young children. A business of this size is still changing, growing and learning new things, but is no longer as messy as the infant. Small businesses have typically found strategies to consistently grow revenues, and have the basic operational infrastructure under-way. The key in this stage is scale. Can they scale what they built? They tend to seek Connectors, Execution Drivers, Task Masters and Problem Solvers.

Medium Business:
$10 Million–$50 Million in Revenue

This is a very fun business stage. Medium businesses are like middle-school kids: They are maturing and finding their rebellious voices. They tend to be a little arrogant, in part because they made it through the previous two stages (start-up and small business), and have experienced some success. Many businesses get stuck in this stage partly because what got them here **is not** what will get them to the next level. Smart businesses bring on experienced management teams now, and the owners move into leadership roles. Those business owners who continue to try to manage the day-to-day activities of a company of this size tend to get stuck here and never realize their potential. There are many opportunities in medium companies. Selecting one with the best cultural fit, and in which there is a competent management team, is paramount. Also, companies of this size tend to seek outside investors, which can change their culture and growth trajectory. Opportunities in this stage are best suited for the following roles: Team Builders, Strategists, Problem Solvers, Task Masters, Game Changers and Execution Drivers.

Large Business:
$50 Million–$100 Million in Revenue

This is a very interesting business stage. The business has shed its adolescent rebellion and settled in to its destiny, strategy and plan. It's probably found a competent management team to support the business founder(s) and may be well positioned for scalability, if well funded. There are two critical components that determine how a company performs in this stage: its ability to build a collaborative team, and its ability to execute its strategy. Often, the company takes on an alter ego and either sees itself as a billion-dollar business, and consequently starts to act like one, or it prefers its small-business roots and tends to cycle through old strategies, without growing at the same trajectory. It's vital for professionals to understand which of those personas the small business has taken on, as they behave very differently. A company that sees its identity as that of a billion-dollar business tends to be more collaborative, and less political. A company that identifies with its small-business roots can become mired in political battles and unfortunately reward loyalty over performance. As long as the company continues to grow, all roles are equally viable, and job security is much more stable.

Suggested Resources

Now that you've mapped out some career options and developed a career strategy, here are some suggested resources for professionals who want to maximize the New World of Work.

If you're not sure whether you should head down the path to being a virtualpreneur, solopreneur or entrepreneur, there are two great training programs to assist you.

1. **VIRTUALPRENEUR UNIVERSITY**
   www.VirtualpreneurUniversity.com

2. **For new entrepreneurs we recommend LAUNCH ON PURPOSE™ www.launchonpurpose.com.**

Also, Succeed on Purpose has a job re-training and placement arm called Talent on Purpose that trains professionals in how to reinvent their careers.

• • •

We hope this chapter has been instrumental in assisting you in mapping out a career strategy to maximize the New World of Work. Despite high national unemployment figures and constant media hype, there is an avalanche of work opportunities for professionals who are willing to think differently about their careers. Never before have there been no boundaries and no limitations to career options. With career personas, role-based hiring strategies and virtualpreneur training options, you can capitalize on the New World of Work!

"If you want something better, you have to be willing to do something different." —*Terri Maxwell*

So far, we've covered a lot of practical issues. What types of skills are needed to succeed? What types of tools and procedures are critical for success? However, the big question in the New World of Work can be summed up in one word: Why? Knowing your why, whether you are a company or a professional seeking to navigate this new world, is one of the most important predictors of success.

Move on to the book's final chapter to understand your own **why**.

CHAPTER 16

BUSINESS AND PURPOSE: FIND YOUR WHY

THE MOST IMPORTANT QUESTION for businesses and professionals attempting to navigate the New World of Work isn't where we are going, but why it matters in the first place. As the world changes faster than we can learn about it, one thing remains the same: We are all seeking more meaning in our lives, our careers and our businesses. Businesses that want to compete for talent in the New World of Work marketplace must have a clear answer as to **why they matter**.

Started by a powerful movement called Conscious Capitalism, this new purpose-based trend is a magnet for talent. These businesses, from Whole Foods Market, to The Container Store, to Trader Joe's, to Zappos have created a powerful purpose and a holistic desire to serve and succeed.

Conscious Capitalism is a philosophy based on the belief that a new form of capital holds the potential for enhancing corporate performance while simultaneously serving the greater good. Conscious Capitalism focuses on four pillars of strategy, starting with defining an organization's higher purpose.

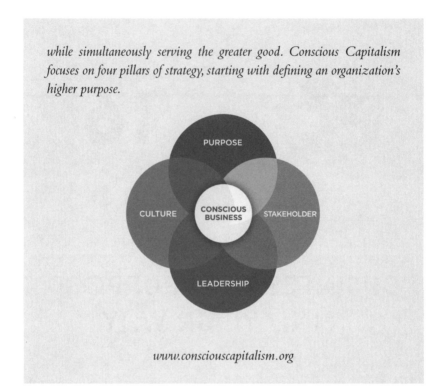

www.consciouscapitalism.org

Purpose is a definitive statement about the difference a business makes in the world. If a company has a purpose and can articulate it with clarity and passion, employees are better able to understand WHY the company exists and how they can add value.

Management is aligned, designs are clear, employees know why their business matters and everyone is clear about how to achieve the purpose. When companies find employees aligned with that purpose, they are intrinsically passionate about the work.

With the New World of Work, businesses can source talent from virtually anywhere. On one hand, it may seem as if the business has the power. However, the real benefit of the New World of Work is that talent can find work anywhere. There are no boundaries to job searches, and you can literally pick up projects globally. The best talent, both salaried and contract, will be attracted to companies that have a clear sense of purpose—a clear why.

A Working Solution

Liz Marx, owner of social media solutions provider <u>nsitesocial.com</u> loves the way she works because she gets to choose projects where she feels she can make the biggest contribution to her company. She can reject projects that she does not align with, especially where social media is concerned. She creates her own schedule. As she put it, she would rather "run lean" on occasion and have the flexibility in her schedule, as opposed to having an eight-to-five workday on a fixed paycheck. The upside is she can add to her schedule if she wants extra income, come to a client's rescue or take advantage of an opportunity to be part of something big and exciting coming down the pipeline. The decision is hers.

"For example, this week is insane, but I created the insanity," she says. "The client called, I looked at my calendar (knowing what was going on) and I said yes. But at least I am not in a situation where a manager comes to me with the kind of request that makes me say, are you kidding me? Do they even know what I do? Obviously someone up there used some kind of logic they can't explain, handed down a request that has implications they couldn't possibly understand. It really makes you wonder what they were thinking."

She goes on to say that she would rather work sixty-five hours virtually than forty hours in a big corporation, because that time belongs to her—to manage as she wishes.

"The time is mine, she says. "If I want to watch my kid's soccer game at 2 p.m. on Monday afternoon, then I can schedule it in."

What Happened to the Iron Triangle?

The election cycles of the last decade have focused on job creation as if government could magically create jobs. Historically, our modern concept of professional employment has been dying since about 1980, as the industrial economy gave way to the Information Revolution.

With this, the model of secure full-time employment is dead. Let's face that fact.

Businesses will save money by drawing upon a global workforce, usually at contractor rates. The publishing houses and the movie studios have been doing this for decades; we call it a networking organization. They bring on specialized talent, complete the project, and then move on to the next project with the next set of specialized workers. —John Slocum, SMU Emeritus Professor, Author of Demystifying Your Business Strategy, Routhledge, 2013, *Professional Business Management Consultant*

The Industrial Revolution created what MSN *Money* magazine refers to as the *Iron Triangle*.

THE IRON TRIANGLE

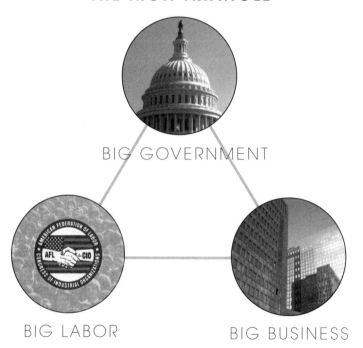

BIG GOVERNMENT

BIG LABOR

BIG BUSINESS

The Iron Triangle is a combination of big business, big government and big labor. The Industrial Revolution created U.S. dominance of the world economy, and consequently a demand for workers.

Government, trying to leverage its world power, assumed that most people would work in large, regulated enterprises that could be compelled or induced to provide pensions, health insurance and other protections. This worked, at the time, because we were only competing against other developed nations, most of who had higher taxes and social protections for workers.

The good news is that more than one billion people worldwide escaped crippling poverty, and companies were equipped with an army of labor. The bad news is that this system is dead, and most companies and workers don't realize it.

In a dynamic, globally competitive world, high-cost producers are doomed. Those countries, particularly the U.S., have seen declining high-wage union jobs for several decades. Conversely, new upstart economies (for example, China, India and Brazil) are not only exceeding at job creation, but are now equipped with a whole new set of tools in the New World of Work.

It is because of these new economies that so many Americans have feared globalization. However, globalization is now the norm. There are no boundaries to work, job creation or talent management.

In this book we have tried to outline real solutions to the lost Iron Triangle era and have encouraged a new way of thinking about public education, corporate talent strategies and work management. In the new age, most jobs will be contractors or temps, and self-employment will become the norm. This requires governments capable of articulating this new strategy and a pioneering group of companies and leaders who can chart the course for the new way of work.

It is because of this revolutionary shift that it is imperative to find your why. It is mission-critical for companies to know why they exist, and how their business serves.

There are several excellent examples of great companies—some of whom are clients of ours—who have identified their purpose and reiterate that purpose in everything they do.

One example is Southwest Airlines. No longer the scrappy little airline that is fighting the big boys, Southwest has become one of the most successful airlines in history. If employees of Southwest are asked, they will say that they are in the business of freedom, not air travel. This purpose is restated in everything from TV commercials to on-plane announcements. Other examples include Barnes & Noble, which is in the business of reading, not books, and Nike, which is in the business of performance, not shoes.

Professionals and Purpose

For professionals, you too MUST find your why. You must know your purpose. Your purpose is who you are, whereas your job is just what you do. Evaluating strengths and passions forms the basis of a Purpose Statement. At what do you truly excel? What are you passionate about? How does it serve?

The more clearly you understand your purpose—your why—the easier it will be to evaluate work opportunities as you chart your path in the New World of Work.

Purpose isn't something you do when you retire. Purpose is who you are.

Your purpose was the same when you were a six-year-old, and was what probably attracted you to a particular field of study in college. If most of us had been left alone to follow our passions, our careers would have looked dramatically different. Your purpose will be the same when you die. The question is whether or not we will live our purpose inbetween our life and our death.

Purpose is your personal and professional why. It's who you are, and it's what you're meant to bring the world. It's your unique gift, and it can be the best compass for charting a path in this New World of Work.

Laura Ermini's path to purpose began when she was young. Inspired by foreign language exposure in a local ethnic neighborhood, she knew she wanted to travel and speak to different people. What she wanted to "do," however, couldn't be corporately compartmentalized. So, she did what society told her to do—go to college, get a job and climb the corporate ladder. Ten years later, she was a successful, award-winning, certified project manager, tethered to a desk. But she was exhausted and deflated. Society and the corporate agenda said she was "doing the right thing."

Laura knew in her heart that just couldn't be right. That's when the shift began.

The problem wasn't the well-lit golf-course-facing office, a particular company or a particular project managerial job. It was ALL of it. The corporate life was no longer fulfilling or sustaining, or at least it wasn't for Laura. She realized that being told when to be somewhere, how much salary she was worth or how many days she could be away from the office was all too constraining.

At one point in her past, she had additional pages sewn into her passport; that same passport has been sitting, untouched, in a drawer, for nearly two years. It was time to get back on the path to purpose!

Laura is outgoing, energetic and enthusiastic. She is confident that she can be more fulfilled, have more fun, move faster, jump higher, accomplish more and live on-purpose by going out on her own. The sacrifices for an every-other-week deposit of cash were too great for her. Paychecks are fed by sacrifice: sacrifice of individuality, time, health, freedom and purpose. Being self-employed does not guarantee a specific salary; it's not about salary. A path on-purpose will be much healthier, enlightening and rewarding.

Now What?

In the 1930s, jobs moved from the farm to the factory. Today, work as we know it has migrated once again. Only this time it has moved from the cube to the cloud.

In the New World of Work, there are no limitations to what, how or where work can be performed. This new world has spawned an entirely new way of **organizing work** and is responsible for innovative business models and career opportunities, all with one thing in common—NO BOUNDARIES.

The New World of Work has leveraged the Information Revolution to transform work and move it from the cube to the cloud. As a result, your business has been transformed, and if you don't develop a strategy to compete for this talent and develop a clear sense of corporate purpose, the best talent will go elsewhere. So, corporate executives, the New World of Work has transformed talent strategies. The question is, have you transformed your business to capitalize on this new world?

Virtualization is happening all around us: work processes, systems, software, hardware, and the list continues. And the exciting part is that it is really just starting. —Andy Geisse, CEO, AT&T Business Solutions

---

Professionals: As a result of the New World of Work, your career has been transformed. The question is: Have you been transformed? Will you continue to search for jobs the old way, or chart new career strategies to maximize your purpose and create roles you can be passionate about? Are you looking for the jobs you lost, or are you reinventing yourselves to maximize this new world?

In the New World of Work, there are no boundaries. There are only opportunities. They may appear different—and possibly scarier—than those of the past because they *are* different. However, they don't have to be scary, not when you're prepared.

The companies and professionals who maximize a boundary-less world of work will be able to teach and lead because they are not afraid of moving ahead.

We hope this book has helped you understand and appreciate our continuing and thrilling leap into the future. If you—as either a professional or business owner—embrace the New World of Work, you are destined to become one of its leading citizens.

ABOUT THE AUTHORS

Tim Houlne

Tim Houlne is a visionary whose long-standing, futuristic predictions about the virtual workforce are now a reality. He recognizes and understands trends, and uses that unique knowledge to transform industries across the business landscape. His understanding of the virtual workplace is unparalleled, and his drive to uncover new concepts is matched only by his passion for growing profitable businesses. Tim holds the position of CEO at Working Solutions, a premier virtual agent and technology solutions provider in Dallas, Texas. He is also a board member for Vision Bank and Chairman of the Movie Institute, a 501(c)3 non-profit organization.

Tim has authored multiple articles and white papers covering a wide-range of subjects including: "Top Traits of High Caliber Agents," "Platform as a Service" and "Contact Center Security—Moving to the Cloud." He is a highly sought-after speaker for industry conferences, business summits and schools. His passion is helping others embrace new concepts and ideas that improve the lives of working professionals while ensuring excellent bottom-line results.

Terri Maxwell

Terri Maxwell provides game-changing insights that transform businesses, people and industries. She is an impactful speaker and passionate leader known for creating successful business models and inspiring the potential of those around her. In a career that spans more than twenty years, Terri put her talents to work for large and small companies, and is a well-known consultant to small businesses and entrepreneurs seeking to accelerate growth.

Throughout her career, Terri has delivered sound solutions to large and small companies, producing unprecedented results and igniting growth. She's launched more than twenty start-up brands, built numerous successful companies and created a well-known and highly respected business incubator, Succeed on Purpose® Inc. in Irving, Texas.

She is the author of *Succeed on Purpose: Everything Happens for a Reason,* a book teaching how to use life's challenges to uncover your purpose.

INDEX

Italic page numbers indicate material in tables or figures.

G

Gallup survey on lack of jobs, 16

Game Changer role, 149

GE (General Electric), 97

Geisse, Andy, 160

Generation Y/Millennials, 58, 100

Genesys, 19, 61, 73–74

George, Alex, 66

Georgetown University, 125

Getaroom.com, 26, 72–73

Gigwalk, 107

Global Consumer Research Study (2011), 35–36

globalization of talent

    defined, 10, 140

    movement of work, 26–28

    as the new norm, 157

    recruitment and, 54, 134–135

    rise of global workers, 15, 17

Google, 19, 67

    empowerment through, 39

    and "learn as you go" culture, 121

    product searches through, 40

graphic designers, 20

Great Depression, 9

Great Recession, 92

H

Harvard University, 127

health care management certificate programs, 126

health insurance, 88, 98

Heard, Kimmie, 48

Hewlett-Packard, 19, 48

high-speed Internet access, 63

HITs (Human Intelligence Tasks), 108

home agent model, 107–108

home offices, 25, *28*, 47, 91, 110

    productivity in, 47

Hostess Brands, 117

Hotels.com, 72–73

Hsieh, Tony, 38

Human Intelligence Tasks (HITs), 108